THE LEADER UPHEAVAL *Handbook*

Lead Teams on an Innovation
& Collaboration Journey
with The 3-4-5 Method™

MICHELE DESTEFANO

AMERICANBARASSOCIATION
ABA Publishing

Cover design by Carolina Martinez/ABA Design

Printed in the United States of America.

27 26 25 24 23   5 4 3 2 1

Library of Congress Cataloging-in-Publication Data

Names: DeStefano, Michele, author.
Title: The leader upheaval handbook : lead teams on an innovation and
    collaboration journey with the 3-4-5 method / Michele DeStefano.
Description: Chicago, IL : American Bar Association, [2023] | Summary:
    "This handbook is designed for the believers: the leader-managers who
    believe that collaboration and innovation are essential to their
    business and who want to learn how to facilitate it; the leader-managers
    who believe that in the process of learning how to collaborate and
    innovate, professional service providers begin to hone the much-needed
    skillsets and mindsets that delight clients. It is designed for the
    leader-manager who is tired of the design thinking methods that are
    messy and confusing and not geared toward professional service
    providers' temperament, training, and current ways of working. And for
    those who desire to lead multidisciplinary teams on a collaborative,
    innovation journey and who seek a method that is methodical, clear, and
    proven successful among professionals who have no prior training in
    design thinking or innovation"-- Provided by publisher.
Identifiers: LCCN 2023015047 (print) | LCCN 2023015048 (ebook) |
    ISBN 9781639053476 (paperback) | ISBN 9781639053483 (epub)
Subjects: LCSH: Practice of law--Social aspects--United States. |
    Leadership--United States. | Success in business--United States.
Classification: LCC KF300 .D4735 2023 (print) | LCC KF300 (ebook) |
    DDC 340.023/73--dc23/eng/20230719
LC record available at https://lccn.loc.gov/2023015047
LC ebook record available at https://lccn.loc.gov/2023015048

Discounts are available for books ordered in bulk. Special consideration is given to state bars, CLE programs, and other bar-related organizations. Inquire at Book Publishing, ABA Publishing, American Bar Association, 321 N. Clark Street, Chicago, Illinois 60654-7598.

www.shopABA.org

Contents

Introduction

This handbook is an accompaniment to my books[1] *Leader Upheaval* and *Legal Upheaval*. It is designed for inclusive, adaptive leader-managers who have already read one of these books and have taken the recommended steps to hone their own skills and mindsets and develop the right processes for a culture of collaboration and innovation to thrive. It is designed for those who don't have to be convinced of the importance of collaboration and innovation to client-centricity and culture creation.

This book is designed for the leader-managers who are tired of the design thinking methods that are messy and confusing and not geared toward professional service providers' temperament, training, and current ways of working.

This book is designed for those who desire to lead multidisciplinary teams on a collaborative, innovation journey and who seek a method that is methodical, clear, and proven successful among professionals who have no prior training in design thinking or innovation.

If all of that describes you, this handbook is for you.

This handbook, and the method it is based on, is the fruit of 13 years of my experience leading more than 230 multidisciplinary, multicultural, and intergenerational teams on a 4-month innovation journey—from problem to viable solution. Utilizing a process I have developed over the years, known as The 3-4-5 Method™, through my consultancy MOVELΔW and LawWithoutWalls,[2] I have helped teams made up of business professionals, attorneys, entrepreneurs, and law and business school students from around the world collaborate to solve a business or social responsibility challenge.

Although my focus has been on innovation, The 3-4-5 Method™ is just as much—if not more—about client-centricity, collaboration, and culture change. This is because the Method's primary design is changing the mindsets, skillsets, and behaviors of professional service providers. As such, it is a method that delivers upskilling (teaches additional skills to help professionals do their job) and re-skilling (teaches a new set of skills in order to perform a different job) related to proactive co-collaboration, client-centricity,

---

[1] This handbook is designed to accompany either of the author's other books *Legal Upheaval* (ABA Publishing, 2018) and *Leader Upheaval* (forthcoming).

[2] See www.lawwithoutwalls.org.

and creative problem finding and solving. It is a method to move teams from symptoms to root causes and from a focus on expertise to *experiences*. And along the journey, it transforms relationships (especially those between professionals and clients).

I know from my experience (as an advertising executive, attorney, consultant, and professor) that motivating professional service providers to collaborate, innovate, and change is not easy—and definitely not "as easy as 1-2-3." But this handbook makes it as easy as 3-4-5. With real examples, it brings to life a method that can be completed in 3 Phases, over 4 months or less, with 5 Steps. It provides practical tips and tools for leading a collaborative, innovation journey so that teams move from a thorny problem to what I call a Project of Worth: which consists of a viable solution plus the added benefit of the cultivation of new mindsets and skillsets among team members. This handbook also provides week-by-week detailed instructions as to how to create the right teaming climate, facilitate project development and run team meetings specifying the exercises teams should conduct to ensure that the right deliverables are accomplished on time and incompetent failure is avoided. As such, it serves as a train-the-trainer "instructor's manual" for leader-managers. Although this handbook provides instructions for a 4-month journey, The 3-4-5 Method™ can be used in any time frame to help teams collaborate on solving a problem or seizing an opportunity of any kind or size, whether that is developing a three-year strategy, creating a more effective and efficient process for billing clients, or designing an innovative tech tool to enhance knowledge sharing. As such, this handbook makes the process of leading multidisciplinary teams accessible to any leader for any type of collaborative problem-solving initiative in professional services.

## CHAPTER 1

An Overview of The 3-4-5 Method™: Why, What, and How

A.   WHY THE 3-4-5 METHOD™ WAS CREATED

"Though this be madness, yet there is method in't."[1]

POLONIUS in HAMLET

I hope that, after you have read my other books, *Leader Upheaval: A Guide to Client-Centricity, Culture Creation, and Collaboration*[2] and *Legal Upheaval*,[3] I have already convinced you that the art of collaboration and innovation starts with you. It is only after you, the leader, emulate the mindsets and behaviors of an inclusive, adaptive leader (the mindsets and skillsets on the Professional Skills Delta featured in Figure 1.1), that you will convince others to follow suit. And even if you have successfully applied the recommendations from my book on creating the right (safe, inclusive) climate, granting the right permissions, developing the right procedures for a culture of collaboration to thrive, the rub is that the leader needs to convince each potential member of each multidisciplinary team to join the problem-solving, innovation journey with an open, growth mindset. And to do that with professional service providers? You need to sell it differently than design thinking has been sold before. And you need to lead it differently as well.

While it is true that all innovation processes include a little messiness, trying to manage any collaborative problem-solving journey or innovation initiative without a method is

---

[1] WILLIAM SHAKESPEARE, HAMLET act 2, sc. 2, l. 205.

[2] MICHELE DESTEFANO, LEADER UPHEAVAL: A GUIDE TO CLIENT-CENTRICITY, CULTURE CREATION, AND COLLABORATION (ABA Publishing, forthcoming 2023).

[3] MICHELE DESTEFANO, LEGAL UPHEAVAL: A GUIDE TO CREATIVITY, COLLABORATION, AND INNOVATION 241–65 (ABA Publishing, 2018).

madness. However, when it comes to innovation and design thinking, it is often presented as a messy almost nonprocess, with overlapping iterative spaces that, frankly, aren't easily understood by those who were not formally educated in innovation and design thinking. Think about it. There are many lawyers, accountants, insurance brokers, and IT professionals who graduated with their respective expert degrees having never had to truly collaborate on a team project and having never taken a course on collaboration, innovation, or design thinking. Further, unless they attended business school, likely the majority (if not all) of their grades and assessments were based on individual contributions (not team). Furthermore, the firms in which they now work are likely more individualistic and competitive and discourage risk taking and encourage conformity—and the professionals often are assessed based on their own contributions and, in some industries, based on billable hours or individual commissions. This means there is an inherent lack of extrinsic motivation to collaborate well on an innovation journey. Therefore, the emphasis that many design thinking methods place on how iterative and unpredictable and prone to failure innovation journeys are can be off-putting to professional service providers who, as described in my other books, are often risk averse, analytical, and methodical.[4] If they can't see the reason for it and they are put off, then they lack not only extrinsic motivation but also intrinsic motivation.

Further, consider that, if you haven't been trained to ideate in the way design thinkers do, the process can be uncomfortable, difficult, and, unfortunately, unsuccessful. Group ideation sessions in which people gather around a white board (virtually or in-person), act silly, and are required to think on the spot—or, worse yet, put all the thoughts on a bunch of Post-it® notes to be placed on the board—are antithetical to how many professional service providers prefer to think and ideate. They prefer to work behind closed doors, often solo, and almost always rationally and objectively—with a concentration on converging on an answer. Being asked to employ methods that require empathy and emotional connection with users and that prevent teams from quickly identifying a solution can seem overly subjective and inefficient.[5] And having to squeeze brilliant thoughts into one or two words on a sticky note isn't how many professional service providers prefer to communicate. Not to mention the fact that this is also antithetical to how introverts work and therefore is not inclusive. This is unfortunate because this format isn't necessary for collaboration or innovation efforts to succeed, although it seems part and parcel of many methods.

Also, many methods do not identify how or when to move from one stage to another in the ideation process or who should be doing what. They also do not delineate timeframes and role identification, nor do they differentiate competent from incompetent failure. Professional service providers are paid for their knowledge, expertise, and time. This is true even if they charge a flat rate vs a billable hour, and even if they work internally within a company vs at an external firm. Any time that they are not working with or for a client is

---

[4] DESTEFANO, *supra* note 2 and note 3.

[5] Christian Bason & Robert D. Austin, *The Right Way to Lead Design Thinking*, HARV. BUS. REV. (March-April 2019), https://hbr.org/2019/03/the-right-way-to-lead-design-thinking.

unleveraged, invaluable time. I often hear professional service providers say that their firm is doing so well, they don't have time to collaborate or innovate.[6] Convincing them to go on an innovation journey without a real method (without a process) to get them from A to Z and without transparent time boundaries is super hard. They don't have the time or patience and they are eager to rush to solve (which, as discussed at great length in my other books, can lead to solving symptoms instead of problems). Without a method explaining what is necessary and how ideation can occur, professional service providers are likely to be skeptical and untrusting and, frankly, unwilling to "play" and collaborate the way that you might want them to. A quote by W. Edwards Deming, a famous American engineer, sums this idea up: "If you can't describe what you are doing as a process, you don't know what you are doing."[7] And professional service providers do not like *not* knowing what they are doing. They like to be buttoned up. And they will not follow a leader who does not seem to know what they are doing. Having a real process overcomes both hurdles.

Thus, a method that *assumes* that professional service providers understand the phases or stages—and assumes that they actually want to complete the phases (because generally I find professional service providers questioning why they have to do this or that)—isn't going to work. Instead, they need a method (and a leader, i.e., YOU) that helps them navigate the journey.[8] They need a leader who educates and convinces them along the way of the importance of collaboration and forces them to commit to a new type of collaboration, regardless of whether gaps exist due to a lack of training, or extrinsic or intrinsic motivation, or a combination thereof. And the leader needs a process so that they can both lead and manage the teams and their project development.

This is why I created The 3-4-5 Method™: a team-based collaboration and innovation process grounded in design thinking principles and constructed especially for professional service providers' temperament, training, and work preferences. It emphasizes the *how* and *who*. Further, it makes the *what* and *when* very clear so that collaboration comes more easily (and perhaps with more certainty in the process) than it might otherwise. The 3-4-5 Method™: gets its name because it is divided into 3 Phases, over 4 months or less, and in 5 Steps. Although the steps are iterative, this method includes instructions and exercises for each step, along with deliverables, role identification, time commitment, and, importantly, a timeline: the series of meetings and activities that must occur among the team and with external advisers along the innovation journey. This method focuses on developing the mindsets and skillsets of an innovator, culture-creation, and

---

[6] Simon Drane and Ben Kent, *The State of Innovation in Professional Services* (2020) at 8–9, https://drive
.google.com/drive/u/0/search?q=drane%20kent, (reporting that firms do not have the right processes, long-term view, or enough time for innovation).

[7] Good Reads, https://www.goodreads.com/quotes/298857-if-you-can-t-describe-what-you-are-doing
-as-a (last visited May 8, 2023).

[8] *Supra* note 5 (studying how 24 senior executives lead major design thinking projects within large private- and public-sector organizations in five countries and finding that key to the success is effective leadership).

setting expectations (i.e., on purpose, goals, accountability, and transparency). It also focuses on *service* innovation, not just products, which is key for many professional service providers who aren't yet interested or don't quite understand what people mean when they talk about *productizing a service*. It also focuses on chunking big problems into narrow bites that can be solved with adaptive innovation (as opposed to big bang disruptive innovation). Armed with this level of information and predictability, professional service providers are willing to put in the time to develop new skills, new mindsets, and new behaviors—not to mention an implementable solution that can be piloted (without a huge investment).

This handbook was written in part because *managing* innovation is critical—and lack of management is one of the reasons collaborative teaming efforts of any kind fail. However, even with good facilitation and management, the process is guaranteed to be a bit less than "streamlined," and it's always going to be difficult and hard. Therefore, I always stress the importance of a method, and in teaching it, I explain that although the 3 Phases go in order and the 5 Steps are generally sequential, they may also be recursive and iterative; that is, insights during Step 3—wherein there is enhanced understanding and empathizing with the key stakeholders—may lead to changes in the problem statement (Step 2), which also may lead to a need for more investigative research (Step 1), which might require additional expertise. Being able to explain the Method as a process is key to convincing professionals to take the time, because in many ways what M.S. Dhoni, a former Indian professional cricketer, is famous for saying is true: "The process is more important than the results. The result is just a by-product of the process. So take care of the process, all the small things, and eventually you will get the desired result."[9]

Some processes and methods are better than others, however. The 3-4-5 Method™ works because it is targeted, predictable, and methodical but also flexible. To that end, it can be used for any type of problem or opportunity that you want teams of diverse professionals to work on, whether that is developing a three-year strategy for the firm, creating a more effective and efficient process for billing clients, or designing an innovative tech tool to enhance knowledge sharing. You name it, this Method will work on it. Additionally, the best part about the Method is that extrinsic and intrinsic incentives are baked into it, including lots of points at which teams can assess progress and either pivot or celebrate without risking incompetent failure.

B.   WHAT IS THE 3-4-5 METHOD™?

At its core, The 3-4-5 Method™ is designed for multi-disciplinary, multidiversity teaming around a discrete challenge or opportunity. It can be used for one team hacking on

---

[9] Lifestyle Desk, *The Process Is More Important Than the Result: M S Dhoni*, Indian Express (Aug. 7, 2019, 11:06 IST), https://indianexpress.com/article/lifestyle/life-positive/ms-dhoni-process-is-more -important-than-the-result-m-s-dhoni-inspiring-video-good-morning-5882798/.

one challenge or multiple teams hacking on multiple challenges. And the "challenges" can be problems needing to be solved, innovations the firm or company wants to create, opportunities yet to be leveraged, processes to be improved, or any other project. In Law-WithoutWalls, we often work with around 15 to 18 teams in each "cohort," which means we have 125 to 170 people involved at some level. Likely, most readers won't be biting off something that big at once. The level of detail in the remaining chapters of this handbook is extreme so that you can apply The 3-4-5 Method™ to your needs and timing—based on your goals, the opportunity or problem you are tackling, and how many teams you are working with at once. This section is simply an overview so that you understand the basic components.

The 3-4-5 Method™ is a team-based experiential collaborative innovation process grounded in design thinking principles. It is constructed especially for professional service providers based on their temperament, training, work preferences, and innovation needs. It makes clear the "how," "who," and "what" so that creativity, collaboration, and innovation come easier than they otherwise might. As mentioned above, the Method is not only about creating solutions. It is also designed to help train the skills on the Professional Skills Delta (including self-awareness, empathy, adaptability, cultural competency, creative problem finding and solving, business planning, communication, and collaboration). See Figure 1.1.

This thereby leads to the development of inclusive leaders who know how to provide client-centric, full-service client service that is focused on the client's experience. The transformation of relationships between clients and professional service providers comes

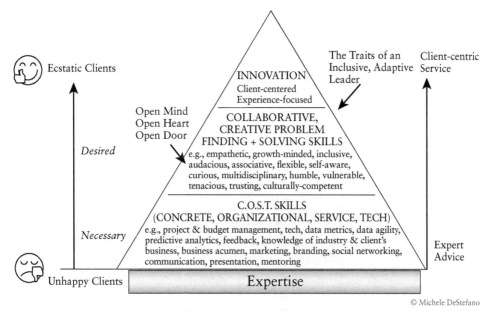

© Michele DeStefano

Figure 1.1 The Professional Skills Delta.

from that development but *more so* if clients are on the teams, included in the journey. At the end of a 3-4-5 journey, in addition to a solution, participants will have developed new skills, new mindsets, and new behaviors. Indeed, this was the original vision of LawWith-outWalls and why I created this method: To develop cross-competent business leaders with excellent creative, collaborative problem finding and solving skills who delight clients by approaching service with the mindset, skillset, and behaviors of innovators. And this is why we call the solutions Projects of Worth because even if the solution is not brought to fruition, there is so much worth in the progress we have made as individuals along the way. So, in following The 3-4-5 Method™, if we really embrace it, as individuals, we cannot fail. Of course, the Method can't *guarantee* that each team will actually create a viable solution that can be brought to life to solve the problem. It can guarantee, however, the change in mindset, skillset, and behaviors talked about above. As long as each person individually commits to the Three Rules of Engagement (discussed at length in my other books) and utilizes the 5 Steps to a Project of Worth, they will have grown as leaders and collaborators. Further, when multiple teams from the same entity go on a 3-4-5 Journey, the Method connects teams across different offices, departments, and practice areas, and fosters a climate for inclusive collaboration and innovation across the entity's business. And, of course, it transforms relationships with clients (internal or external) if they are included as I continually urge.

The Method's name is descriptive. The 3 stands for a process that always (no matter how long) occurs in 3 Phases: (1) a KickOff, (2) multidisciplinary teaming to develop a project, and (3) a ConPosium (pitching presentations to experts to receive feedback and celebrating progress).

Figure 1.2 below depicts the 3 Phases.

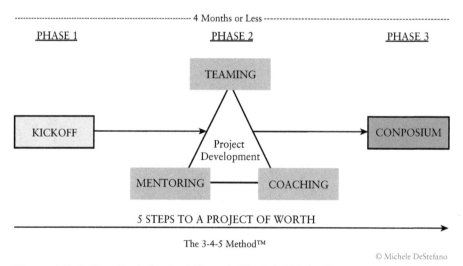

Figure 1.2 A Chart Depicting the 3 Phases in The 3-4-5 Method™.

The 4 stands "for" the period of time that the team sets at the outset for the innovation journeys and for the number 4 as in 4 months or less. (Perhaps it should be named the 3-for-5 Method.) Although the Method has been tested and proved successful in various increments of time (4 months, 3 months, one intense week, 3 days, and 48 hours), the 4 stands for the maximum number of months any innovation journey should exist before it reaches a ConPosium. Does this mean that a project will be fully baked by then? No, but it does mean that a decision about its viability and a business case and marketing plan justifying further development should be prepared and assessed by this time and that progress should be celebrated. As discussed in *Leader Upheaval*, a project lasting longer than 4 months risks incompetent failure of different kinds including burn-out. There is a reason that we have four seasons and that universities around the world work on a semester system wherein semesters are around 4 months long or less.

Just as the phases can be of different lengths of time, they can be done either in-person or virtually. The very first LawWithoutWalls program (LawWithoutWalls Original) was part virtual back in 2011. That's crazy. We were in effect zooming before Zoom! We held our 2-day KickOff in-person in Phase 1, then went virtual during the teaming in Phase 2 (using AdobeConnect and other video conferencing platforms combined with Google Drive). Then, at the end of the 4 months, we met in-person again for Phase 3, The ConPosium. In 2013, we launched our first all-virtual program (LWOW X) where we did all 3 Phases online, including a 48-hour virtual KickOff. The coolest thing about saying that now is that no one understood how exhausting it was; now everyone does! In 2022, we launched LawWithout Walls Sprint, (3 days in-person format), and it was a huge success then and again in 2023. Thus, the Method, although it has structure, has baked-in flexibility.

The 5 stands for the 5 Steps that each team must go through to move from an opportunity or challenge to a solution that has the possibility of viability. Although the steps are iterative, as explained in more detail in Chapter 4, they provide a sequential trajectory for the team to measure its progression.

1. Phase 1: The KickOff (Individual, Team, and Community Building)

Given how much emphasis I place on the importance of having a KickOff in my other books, it will not surprise you to know that Phase 1 in The 3-4-5 Method™ is the KickOff. The KickOff is the most essential ingredient to team success. It creates the culture and sets the protocols and expectations and, even more importantly, creates commitment and accountability at the individual, subgroup, and team levels. The KickOff is designed to meet three goals:

- First, to train participants on The 3-4-5 Method™ and best practices for multicultural, multidisciplinary teaming and collaboration.
- Second, to knit together engaged and committed teams of individuals to create team cohesion and community culture.

- And third, to prepare participants for the personal and professional work ahead and identify and reinforce individual commitment to protocols, rules of engagement, intentions, and goals.

The members of the teams are intentionally diverse in every way possible: culture, discipline, gender, age, expertise, talents, and backgrounds. The entire team is made up of approximately five to nine people with varying, yet very clear delineation of roles, that is, who are the hackers ("doers"), who are the mentors, who are the coaches, and what are their respective expectations. Note: these roles are described in detail in Chapter 2. And importantly, in addition to roles, we identify subteams within the teams. Nine people cannot collaborate all at once! (Recall the emphasis on the importance of thinking tiny in *Leader Upheaval* both in terms of team size and scope of projects.)

At the KickOff, we participate in teaming exercises and we also conduct an expectation-commitment exercise we call *P.A.C.T.s*, designed to ensure the team agrees to purpose and garners commitment and accountability. Importantly, we also provide substantive training about leadership and collaboration and also about design thinking and innovation in general. We review the recipe for creating the right climate as depicted by the acronym S.A.F.E.T.Y. We introduce the Three Rules of Engagement: Open Mind, Open Heart, Open Door (discussed at length in my other books and described briefly in Chapter 3). And then we practice the Three Rules of Engagement. And of course, we provide training about The 3-4-5 Method™ itself.

As to the length and content of a KickOff, that varies based on the number of teams and how long your journey is slated to be. Either way, if there is more than one team involved, it is essential that there is community building across the teams as well as among each individual team. This can be hard (especially in a virtual setting), but it can be done. As discussed in the next chapter, the look, feel, and energy of the KickOff is critical to set the right mood and give license to the participants to try on the new behaviors and mindsets we are trying to further hone from the Skills Delta and bring out their crayons to "play." Therefore, we always pick an aspirational theme for the KickOff and a song that goes with it. Themes around climbing a mountain, going for gold in a relay race, or shooting for the moon work very well and have great songs related to them like "Ain't No Mountain High Enough," "Rocky Mountain High," and "Dancing in the Moonlight."

To further develop community, prior to KickOff, we have individuals record themselves lip syncing to a segment of our KickOff theme song. Then we splice the segments together to create a community lip-sync music video and we play it at the beginning of the KickOff as the first community collaborative endeavor. In watching it together, we begin to transform from individuals to a highly cooperative, socially integrated superorganism similar to a beehive. Why does this work? Research shows that working (walking, singing, chanting) in unison breaks down psychological walls, and creates group cohesion.[10] We do it for the same reasons people sing in church, armies march in unison, dancers dance to the beat. And we don't do it just with a lip sync. At least once during every KickOff, we have all of our participants sing or dance or do some type of mirroring activity together in unison as well.

Another way we develop community building across teams is we assign each team what we call a Shadow Team. Participants meet their Shadow Team at the KickOff but each team's Shadow Team stays with them throughout the entire journey (no matter how long or short).

Shadow Teams are based loosely on the concept of red teams.[11] The term *red team* comes from the practice during the Cold War of having U.S. officers try to "think red" (i.e., like a Soviet Union officer trying to figure out how he might defeat U.S. strategies). U.S. red teams utilized Soviet technology and theory to try to determine how to destroy its own U.S. Navy submarine forces. The thinking is that by learning how to defeat yourself from the enemy's vantage point, you can protect yourself better. (Note: If you are offended by the concept of red teams, it might make you feel better to know that the Soviets did the same thing, calling them blue teams.)

In LawWithoutWalls we call them Shadow Teams instead of red teams because a *shadow* can be a blind spot or is similar to the Jungian definition, something we project but do not yet own. The idea is that the Shadow Teams help fill the gaps on the teams. Their purpose is to play the role of devil's advocate, to find weaknesses or strengths that the team may not be aware of. Although as discussed as part of our Rules of Engagement, we should never stop saying "Yes, and . . . .", we look to the Shadow Team to be our naysayers to assist us in evaluating and reflecting on our projects to develop them further.

2. Phase 2: Teaming through the 5 Steps to a Project of Worth

After the KickOff, teams begin project development. Teaming can occur in-person or virtually or in a combination of the two. Work is done in team meetings within their subgroups and also at times with the other subgroups and external advisors as they progress through the 5 Steps. Through these meetings, teams receive feedback to improve the

---

[10] Scott Wiltermuth & Chip Heath, *Synchrony and Cooperation*, 20 PSYCH. SCI., (2009); Selin Kesebir, *The Superorganism Account of Human Sociality: How and When Human Groups Are Like Beehives*, 16 PERSONALITY AND SOC. PSYCH. REV. 233, 233-261 (2011); *see, e.g.*, Piercarlo Valdesolo et al., *The Rhythm of Joint Action: Synchrony Promotes Cooperative Ability*, 46 J. OF EXPERIMENTAL SOC. PSYCH. 693, 693-695 (2010) (finding that synchronous rocking enhances connectedness); Sebastian Kirschner & Michael Tomasello, *Joint Music Making Promotes Prosocial Behavior in 4-Year-Old Children*, 31 EVOLUTION AND HUM. BEHAV. 354, 354-364 (2010).

[11] Cass R. Sunstein and Reid Hastie, *Making Dumb Groups Smarter*, HARV. BUS. REV., Nov. 2014.

viability, financial structure, and overall positioning and creativity of the project. This is part of the prototyping, testing, reassessing, and improving process.

In LawWithoutWalls, when we are on a 4-month journey journeying with multiple teams, we meet weekly to attend interactive virtual webinars in order to build community across teams. In addition to serving as community building, these webinars serve as substantive training in the Method, as they are focused on topics like consumer storytelling, prototyping, branding, business planning, and more. These webinars are a great way to involve lots of different members of the community (or entice new members) as guest panelists who can share their stories from their own innovation journeys. They are lively and purposefully engaging to incentivize the community to keep in contact and get to know each other. In other modes, for example, when LawWithoutWalls is conducted in-person over the course of a week or three days, we hold these webinars prior to the KickOff.

Phase 2 is when the hard work is done and lots of battles are not won. It is when the teams have to actually apply the Three Rules of Engagement in tough times (as opposed to at a fun KickOff) to move through the 5 Steps to a Project of Worth described below. It is also when teams have to live up to the intentions and protocols that they set at KickOff. And, at times, it is when teams face personal and/or professional and/or cultural divides.

As mentioned above, the "5" in The 3-4-5 Method™ of Innovation stands for the 5 Steps each team must tackle in order to meet its objective: a viable, feasible solution to a defined problem for a discreet target audience along with a prototype, business case, and commercial (some type of 30- to 60-second video that brings the problem and solution, including its brand, to life in a compelling way).

The 5 Steps are as follows:

Step 1: Exploring and Investigating the Challenge
Step 2: Finding and Refining the Problem or Opportunity
Step 3: Understanding Key Stakeholders and Target Audience(s)
Step 4: Solving the Problem and Prototyping
Step 5: Planning, Assessing, and Testing the Solution

I created the 5 Steps after reading about a man named Tim Young who raised $10 million in one year by using just five "magic" slides in his fundraising deck.[12] His reasoning was: "If you can't outline your business in just five slides, you should go back to the drawing board and simplify your messaging."[13] This resonated with me, so I decided to create a method in five steps—so that each step could be a slide if someone was pitching to a venture capitalist. That said, we do not limit our teams to five slides. Instead, we often

---

[12] Tim Young, *365 Days, $10 Million, 3 Rounds, 2 Companies, All with 5 Magic Slides*, TECHCRUNCH (Nov. 2, 2010), https://techcrunch.com/2010/11/02/365-days-10-million-3-rounds-2-companies-all-with-5-magic-slides/.

[13] *Id.*

limit them to an Ignite-style presentation: 20 self-advancing slides in five minutes. And we always tell our teams that they should NOT present the 5 Steps in order. Instead, we recommend they start with a story that describes the size and impact of the problem in a way that moves the audience.

The hardest part about The 3-4-5 Method™ is teams have to repeat steps because they are iterative. They go back and forth. Sometimes, teams take huge steps back and only baby steps forward. Sometimes progress feels chaotic before it feels integrative. There is no certainty that progress will be made from moving from Step 1 to Step 2 or from Step 2 to Step 3 because what teams find in Step 3, can send them back to Step 2. Further, time can be slowed because teams often have to go through some mourning for the ideas they had to let go to move forward. However messy it may appear, the results can often be sublime. The most difficult steps to progress through are Steps 2 and 3. As discussed in great length in *Leader Upheaval* and *Legal Upheaval*, research shows the best problem solvers are the best problem finders. Problems need to be refined and whittled down, and a consumer story (from each point of view) needs to be uncovered and understood. And the team needs to really empathize with the target audience(s) to ensure that the team understands why this problem or opportunity matters, and to ensure that they are solving a real problem (and not a symptom of the problem) for a real target audience. So Steps 2 and 3 take a good portion of the innovation journey and if done right, make Steps 4 and 5 much easier. For detail on each of the 5 Steps, see Chapter 4.

3. Phase 3: The ConPosium (Pitching, Assessing, and Celebrating)

Teams then reconvene in-person or online to pitch their Projects of Worth (dynamic pitch, branded prototype, business case, commercial, and tagline) at The ConPosium, an ending event that has some high stakes. This is why developing your personal brand and a dynamic presentation style is an essential skill on the Skills Delta and something we emphasize in The 3-4-5 Method™. We call this event a ConPosium because it is a quasi-conference/symposium wherein teams present their Projects of Worth to an audience and a panel of expert judges who ask questions and provide feedback. But the ConPosium is much more than simply a set of presentations.

First and foremost, the ConPosium is a community celebration to reunite the community as one, despite the fact that, in some ways, the process may have been a competition. The reality is an entity likely can't bring all teams' projects to life and also, in a journey of 10 teams, it is likely that only two will be baked enough to want to invest in by this time. Yet, all are worth celebrating. And to help the celebratory notion and community building, we create a community ConPosium video that is a combination of video recorded during the KickOff and then also during the ConPosium and spliced together to music and played at the end (often while votes are tallied). People LOVE seeing themselves in action in the video.

Second, the ConPosium is also a form of reflection (of assessing and testing). As part of the 5 Steps to a Project of Worth, the ConPosium is a time for feedback, for testing our prototypes, and for analyzing our business cases. The ConPosium is an opportunity to present the problem, solution, and prototype in front of the community and receive critique from learned experts and from each other. Indeed, we often include a live chat that is featured on a screen in the room so community audience members can provide support to their fellow teams, live feedback on projects, and their own questions or responses to the judges' questions. These chats are saved so they can be reviewed by the presenting team later and used to refine their presentations and Projects of Worth.

Thus, last, and perhaps counterintuitively, the ConPosium, although it is an ending point for the team, is not the end. This might be the hardest part for professional service providers to swallow because the ConPosium feels like the end, so they want to be done. And this can be the case. It can be that other teams take up where the ConPosium teams leave off. However, the only downside to that is the loss of control and influence the original founders of the idea will have. That said, it is likely a good thing for the idea and its implementation to have fresh eyes. So the ConPosium, even if it is an end for the specific individuals, is not an end for the Projects of Worth. It is a continuation of the middle. So despite that the 3 Phases in The 3-4-5 Method™ feel like a beginning, middle, and end, the reality is that they are all middles. As Robert Frost aptly put: "Ends and Beginnings—there are no such things. There are only middles."[14]

C.   HOW TO APPLY THE 3-4-5 METHOD™ AND USE THIS HANDBOOK

At its core, The 3-4-5 Method™ is designed for multidisciplinary teaming around a discrete topic, challenge, or opportunity. Thus, prior to implementing the Method, the recommendations made in my book, *Leader Upheaval*, around honing your own skills and mindsets, creating the right climate, and developing the right processes for a culture of collaboration and innovation to thrive should have been followed. Further, prior to implementation, a Lead Facilitator (who has the skills of the leader manager) must be appointed. For our purposes, this handbook will assume that you, the reader, will be the leader manager who is selected as the Lead Facilitator. That said, for some substantive support, you might consider farming out some of the role to other experts to lower the tax on yourself but also to give the participants a diversity of learning styles.

This handbook serves as the "instruction manual" for leaders who actually want to facilitate or oversee a collaborative journey, whether the goal is innovation, problem solving, or strategic planning. There is this saying in America: "It's as easy as 1, 2, 3." And that's definitely not the case with collaborative journeys. However, with this Method, it is as easy as 3-4-5. It brings to life a method that can be completed in 3 Phases, over 4 months

---

[14] Robert Frost, The Road Not Taken and Other Poems 11 (David Orr ed., 2015).

or less, with 5 Steps. It provides practical tips and tools for leading a collaborative, innovation journey so that teams move from a thorny problem to a Project of Worth. This handbook also provides tips, tools, and week-by-week detailed instructions as to how to create the right teaming climate, facilitate project development, and run team meetings—specifying the exercises teams should conduct to ensure that the right deliverables are accomplished on time and incompetent failure is avoided. As such, it serves as a train-the-trainer "instructor's manual" for leader-managers. The instructions are based on the assumption that there is one overarching Lead Facilitator overseeing all the teams on the journey (whether there are two or more teams). It also assumes that each of the teams has a Project Manager to prevent drift. (A caveat: if there are only a handful of teams on the journey, then the Lead Facilitator could also serve in the Project Manager role.) The instructions in the next few chapters go into great detail, including detailing the prep needed, what to incorporate in the KickOff, how the Project Manager should run team meetings on a weekly basis, what exercises teams they should conduct to create the right collaborative climate and to develop their projects, how and when the Lead Facilitator should run the 5-Step Milestone Meetings, what substantive learning should occur along the way, and how to plan and facilitate the ConPosium. To help bring the directions to life, this handbook also provides real life examples of how projects have developed through each of the 5 Steps in The 3-4-5 Method™. Although this handbook provides instructions for a 4-month (16-week) journey, The 3-4-5 Method™ can be used in any time frame. So, for those who want to facilitate a shorter journey, I have included in the Appendix suggested journey schedules for 4 weeks and 3 days. For those that want more detailed instructions, reading and video recommendations to build substantive expertise and directions for running the recommended weekly exercises can be found on my websites movelaw.com and micheledestefano.com.

Rest assured, The 3-4-5 Method™ can work with any project team or committee assigned to any challenge or opportunity—even if that assignment is to create a forward-looking 3-year strategic plan for the company or firm. As other experts have also found, strategic planning based on analytical tools alone can only go so far.[15] Without a method, tools, or exercises to spark creative thinking, committees are hard pressed to find innovative ways to reshape what has been done in the past or create new, game-changing strategies. The 3-4-5 Method™ is designed to add that creative spark. And as noted, one of the reasons this method is also valuable is that, in the process, it hones the skills and attributes on the Professional Skills Delta noted above—which all, of course, work to enhance client-centricity and to move our focus from the services themselves to the experiences. Before jumping into the instructions for leading an innovation journey, however, we must start with the planning and prep work that needs to be done prior to a journey of any kind.

---

[15] Adam Brandenburger, *Strategy Needs Creativity*, Harv. Bus. Rev. (Mar.-Apr. 2019), https://hbr.org/2019/03/strategy-needs-creativity.

## CHAPTER 2

Planning for a Collaboration or Innovation Journey

In addition to creating the right climate, structure, and processes and identifying a Lead Facilitator, there is other prep work that should be done (and decisions that need to be made) to help the entire journey go more smoothly and ensure a proper KickOff and ConPosium. This chapter focuses on the prep work that is absolutely necessary prior to the Kick-Off. I leave the prep work for the ConPosium until later; however, be aware that some of the ConPosium prep needs to be done early, maybe even now, depending on the length of your journey. This is especially true if your ConPosium will be in-person and widely attended. So be sure to read Chapter 5 before you start as it outlines the prep required and the other details to facilitate a successful ConPosium. This chapter only deals with prep prior to the start of the journey. Chapter 3 provides the detail on how to run the KickOff itself (which occurs during week 1 of the journey). Then Chapter 4 provides a week-by-week breakdown for Phase 2 (weeks 2-15) as teams journey through the 5 Steps to a Project of Worth. The ConPosium that occurs in the final week, the 16th week, is covered in Chapter 5.

The prep work that needs to be done prior to the start of the journey, that is, the Kick-Off, is as follows: (A) Developing a Roadmap (that details the length of the journey, the schedule of Milestone Meetings and deliverables, and the types of technological tools that will be used); (B) Creating The Right Space and Place; (C) Selecting Participants; (D) Identifying Team Project Topics; (E) Creating Teams and Assigning Roles; and (F) Building Community Across the Teams. Below, I have provided an estimate of the timing based on a 4-month journey (and included shorter timing suggestions in the Appendix). However, even if you are going on a 4-month journey beware: KickOff prep timing varies depending on whether it is in-person or virtual. If the KickOff is in-person, then prep should begin at least 12 weeks prior. This is because securing space and people's time (along with other event planning logistics) for an in-person event has a longer lead time than for a virtual one. However, bet on at least 8 weeks of prep time needed before any type of KickOff.

A.   DEVELOPING A ROADMAP

Prior to embarking on the journey, a roadmap should be developed for the entire journey. A decision should be made as to the length of time the journey will last—which as discussed should be no longer than 4 months—the number of teams, and also the key dates including the Kickoff and ConPosium, all the various types of meetings including webinars (as shown below in Figure 2.1) and key deliverables. In fact, no matter how long your journey, I recommend creating this timeline 12 to 8 weeks prior to the start and that you do this prior to selecting participants. That way, participants can account for these dates on their calendar when deciding to participate. In LawWithoutWalls, we go so far as to have all participants sign a document, called a *P.A.C.T.*, committing to their purpose, accountability, creative cadence, and, importantly, TIME, for example, attending the essential meetings as slated in the calendar—and we send calendar invites immediately to hold the time. We don't send calendar requests for the weekly team meetings of course, because each team needs to choose those times based on the personal and professional lives of the team; but we do it for the 5-Step Milestone Meetings, substantive Webinars, KickOff, and ConPosium. Participants also need to know—in advance of committing— the format and location of the KickOff and ConPosium, that is, if virtual, what platform, if in-person, what location. See Figure 2.1.

Also, I recommend that you have something that harkens to a pre-prepared syllabus, that is, a *Master Planner* that outlines all the deliverables and goals, along with the extra substantive resources you will provide along the journey. In addition to assigning a mix of articles or books to read and short videos to watch, I recommend hosting approximately five to eight live or prerecorded webinars (delivered by experts) that provide substantive training on how to move through the steps and that bring the 5 Steps to life. It's hard to create a consumer story if you haven't learned about the art of storytelling and seen a few great examples of consumer stories brought to life. The same is true for business planning and prototyping. A *Sample 4-Month Journey Master Planner* (i.e., "syllabus") is available on my websites (movelaw.com and micheledestefano.com) that mirrors all the recommendations in this handbook and includes recommended readings, as well as videos and webinars. Of course, this "syllabus" can be used to create shorter or longer journeys.

Last, some advance decisions need to be made on the technology that the teams will use. It is best if you have a collaborative workspace where teams can place their work without version issues, along with channels for chats to share knowledge within teams and across teams, and a preselected video conferencing platform. And of course, it is always best if the Lead Facilitator has the ability to access all teams' work at any time. Therefore, as long as security is not an issue, I recommend using Google Drive along with one chat app that also has video conferencing capability, such as Microsoft Teams or Slack. Although lots of people prefer Zoom, that means there is yet one more tech platform that has to be accessed. A huge pain point for teams is too many platforms! I also recommend creating

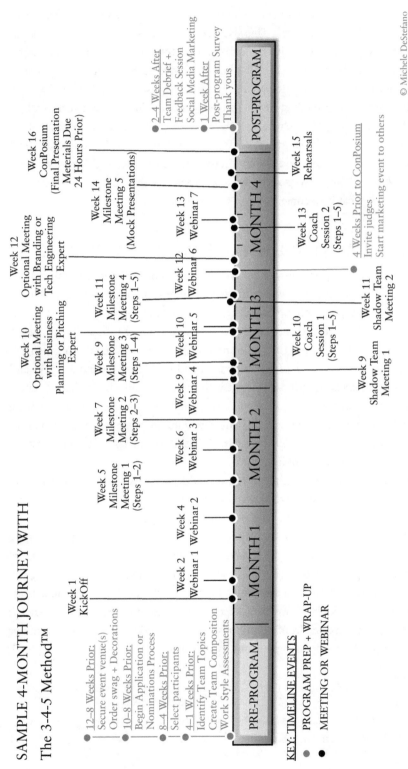

Figure 2.1 A sample 4-month calendar utilizing The 3-4-5 Method™.

the teams' Google Drive folders (and subfolders) and team chat channels in advance so that they can be introduced from day 1. This also helps the teams stay organized from the get-go. However, I would wait to train the teams on the tech until the first team meeting because participants can be overwhelmed. It's best to limit the amount of prep work they will have to do since, generally, participants have day jobs. Just completing a work-style assessment along with some reading on the project topic assigned to the team will be plenty (and likely many people won't do prep work prior to the KickOff anyway!). That said, I also like to provide at least one article on design thinking and a couple optional readings about culture, teaming, and the innovator's mindset. Although many will not read them, for those that are nervous about what to expect, these resources can help calm and prepare them for what is to come.

B.   CREATING THE RIGHT SPACE AND PLACE

Just as what we wear can impact how we behave, where we collaboratively problem solve can too. And I'm not the only one who believes that time should be spent creating the space and place for the type of collaboration that is required in an innovation journey and especially at the KickOff. The goal is to create what Ray Oldenburg calls a "Third Place," which is an environment that is not the home and not the office that enables people from diverse backgrounds and cultures, of different ages, and with different experiences and talents to interact and exchange ideas.[1] Evidently, this is why Vienna flourished. According to Steven Johnson, it was a city, created in large part by Sigmund Freud, to enable physicians, philosophers, and scientists to share thoughts on psychoanalysis.[2] Similarly, the cafes of Paris served as third places during the 1920s for scientists, engineers, writers, artists, and workers to cross-pollinate ideas.

Companies purposefully create third places for multidisciplinary teams to collaborate for this very reason. They understand that when you are asking people to behave differently, you need to create a new space with new rules of engagement to do so. For example, Mattel created an unstructured studio outside of headquarters designed to inspire creative thinking and new collaborative behavior to enable a new product development process—and like recommended in The 3-4-5 Method™, they too do playful teaming and ideation exercises that work to open the minds, hearts, and doors of those participating.[3] At the LawWithoutWalls KickOff, we always have some kind of exercise to leverage the power of play (e.g., build a duck from a random selection of LEGO bricks in less than one minute or a rock-paper-scissors competition). Additionally, as mentioned in Chapter 1,

---

[1] Ray Oldenburg, The Great Good Place: Cafés, Coffee Shops, Community Centers, Beauty Parlors, General Stores, Bars, Hangouts and How They Get You Through the Day 42 (1989).

[2] Steven Johnson, Where Good Ideas Come From: The Natural History of Innovation 159–163 (2010).

[3] Lisa Bannon, *Mattel's Project Platypus Aims to Inspire Creative Thinking*, The Wall St. J. (June 6, 2002), https://www.wsj.com/articles/SB1023305181289347920.

we follow the Three Rules of Engagement: Open Mind, Open Heart, Open Door, which may sound corny but, as discussed in my other books and exemplified by the LawWithoutWalls' community, the rules work to create an inclusive culture of creativity, collaboration, and innovation.

To be clear, a third place does not need to be an offsite location (unless your company or firm does not have event space). However, the look and feel of the room (wherever it is located), including how people sit, matters. And I don't mean changing the seating from audience-style to big round tables. Those round tables serve as obstructions to collaboration. They facilitate heads down work on paper (or on laptops) and spatial distance between people. Instead, the seating should encourage closeness, like when you sit around a fire pit. And it should discourage people from using a laptop or tablet (i.e., working on their own) or having a phone out. At the LawWithoutWalls KickOff, we sit people in a circle with a very small container in the middle that is related to the theme of the KickOff and that can serve as a quasi-coffee table and hold the team's phones and items we want the teams to use later. For example, during the LawWithoutWalls Sprint in 2022, the theme was a race. Our tagline was "Going for the Gold," and our song was "Gold on the Ceiling" by the Black Keys. We decorated drink coolers with gold spray paint and placed them in the center of each team. In each cooler-container, we included any supplies needed for the Sprint activities (markers, Post-its® instructions) and after each break, we placed a gift inside as an incentive for people to exchange their phones, that is, we asked everyone to put their phones INSIDE the cooler so that they were really "there" for the journey and not checking emails or messages. In years past, we have used spaceship-themed backpacks, mountaineering-themed duffle bags, etc. And the swag/tchotchkes we give away are branded and themed e.g., retro-headbands if the theme is a race to the finish theme, or mountain climbing metal clips if the theme is climbing a mountain. My experience (which is also supported by research) shows that the color of the walls, the views from the windows, and the music that is played impact creativity and collaboration.[4]

Thus, there are many ways to make the space more inviting to encourage different and new behavior, for example, the use of couches instead of chairs, walls you can write on, decals on the walls to create a theme (and that look great as backdrops in photos for use in social media), easels to encourage collaborative work, toys like LEGOs or Play-Doh to encourage creativity and play—and of course inspiring music throughout (not just one song for the lip sync). We play music during thinking time and during breaks. You can't just give permission for people to behave differently or to play, you have to make it unavoidable and irresistible. This includes making sure to communicate the right dress code. Suits and ties, skirts and heels do not lend themselves well to the type of collaboration and play you want to encourage at a KickOff and beyond. Neither do formal titles on name tags. Of course it is ideal if this third place can be used throughout the journey for

---

[4] TINA SEELIG, IN GENIUS: A CRASH COURSE ON CREATIVITY 95–102 (2012).

in-person teaming, however, most teams do not have that luxury so spend the time to do it right at the KickOff location.

One other note to keep in mind? There should be no observers during the journey except at the ConPosium. Other than the Lead Facilitator, anyone who attends the KickOff or any Milestone Meeting on a go-forward must be someone who has an assigned role on a team or is contributing to or aiding that team in some way. When observer nonparticipants attend, it makes the team "players" uncomfortable and sets a hierarchy that can trigger negative emotions or worse. This happens all the time. My sponsors in LawWithoutWalls often ask to bring along someone senior to "watch," and I say absolutely not. The same is true for the law firms and legal departments that I consult with and facilitate innovation journeys for. Often the managing partner of the firm wants to attend but not be put on a team. I have learned the hard way that this is not a good idea. It can also cause major damage to the effectiveness of the KickOff. The one time it happened (after my repeated warnings to my client NOT to allow this person to attend) at a KickOff was a complete disaster. Now this managing partner was tragically just like you might imagine when you think "managing partner of a law firm." He interrupted all the time. He talked off point. He went on tangents. He repeated his own ideas. And he repeatedly derailed the work the teams were trying to do. And as for the mood, that is, the space? He was a complete buzz kill.

In addition to the kind of space described above, there is another type of "space" that needs to be considered and that is the space—as in time—in people's schedules. We talked about extrinsic motivations. Asking people to attend a full-day KickOff (and all the other Milestone Meetings shown in the calendar, Figure 2.1 above) might be a stick vs a carrot given the time involved. Think through how you can help the participants protect their time so they can really give their time when they are at the KickOff or in the meetings. Having a senior person explain that this is a priority can help. Having a senior person commit to and attend and actually participate on a team the whole day (and from then on) is even better.

Of course, the best way to garner people's time is to include clients at the KickOff and, even better, also include clients in the journey and on the teams in defined roles. There is no better extrinsic motivator for professional service providers than the opportunity to spend time with a key client. To that end, when planning the KickOff specifically, think through and pre-plan the timing of the breaks, the food and drinks, to ensure there is time and sustenance for casual, organic networking. And let the participants know the KickOff schedule in advance, when there will be breaks. This is important for busy individuals who have clients and families and other life matters that need attending to. I suggest sending all participants a calendar invite for each KickOff session and the breaks. That said, I do not recommend delineating the content or purpose of each session as some participants might selectively choose not to attend a portion, especially if they think they have to participate in "icebreakers"—not that!

One last point. Creating the right place and space is just as important—maybe even more important—if the journey is an all-virtual one. Even though less lead time is needed (compared to an in-person event), it is also more difficult. However, it can be done by creative use of virtual backgrounds, music, and dress code (think costumes and themes and yes! I have dressed up as Albert Einstein, Mozart, and Wonder Woman to help inspire others to get out of themselves. We also created a LawWithoutWalls-Box-Of-Awesome in which we sent participants swag ahead of time that could be worn or used during the KickOff, key Milestone Meetings, and ConPosium to create a community spirit!). But, of course, you need to do what is within the bounds of your culture and your own personal brand (one of those key C.O.S.T. skills on the Professional Skills Delta). That said, don't stay too inside the boundaries or you won't move people into the right "space" to think and behave differently. Also, cool, collaborative tech tools like Mural, Miro, Jamboard, Figma, and Padlet can help as well. Not to mention that there are lots of different cooler and more effective video conferencing platforms than Zoom or Teams, such as Minerva's Forum, Adobe Connect, and AirMeet, that enable more and different interaction and enhanced control over the participant experience (vs participants being able to change the size of the pictures or shut their cameras off, etc.). I highly recommend using a better platform, at least for a virtual KickOff. Plus, many platforms are free for a short trial, so it is not a huge investment in dollars—but it can be a big investment in time to learn the platform of course. Consider this: Pretty soon we will have the ability to do virtual meetings with virtual reality technology and avatars too! If you are doing a virtual KickOff, then pretraining on the tech is essential. That said, if it will create dissonance because learning new tech is problematic, then stick with the video platforms you and the participants are familiar with.

If the KickOff is in-person and some people cannot attend, I do NOT recommend piping them in via Zoom or Teams. I have yet to see a well-run hybrid event wherein some people attend a KickOff in-person and some attend on a video screen. Generally, the folks on video feel out of it, excluded, and awkward. (That said, there might be one small session during the KickOff wherein it makes sense for those who cannot attend to pipe in virtually, e.g., during the Talent and Topic Exploration or P.A.C.T. sessions.) But watching your team do silly teaming exercises through a rabbit hole on someone's tablet is a sure-fire way to have the opposite of a teaming effect for that person, and all your efforts to create the right place and space will be for naught.

Last, don't forget that you need to know the size of your community (how many people and how many teams) AND the length of your KickOff before you can pick a space (in-person or virtual) because the number of people (and days) impacts the ability of the space to accommodate your needs.

So. Whether you are hosting a virtual or an in-person KickOff, hopefully you see why it is essential to start 8 to 12 weeks in advance!

C. SELECTING PARTICIPANTS

Depending on your priorities, there are a few things to think about when selecting the participants for the journey. First, as mentioned above, timing is critical. People need some real lead time if they are going to commit to an innovation journey that is longer than a week. So be sure to begin this process 10 to 8 weeks prior, and select participants at least 8 to 4 weeks prior.

Second, as talked about at great length in my prior books, it is essential to consider how you can multiply the diversity on the teams—which is one of the key ingredients to creative, collaborative problem solving. And I mean diversity of all kinds: race, religion, culture, age, expertise, discipline, economic background, experience, talents—you name it. That said, it is essential that you remember what was emphasized in *Leader Upheaval* about team size. Too many professionals sit on too many committees that are too large to be effective—even with sub-groups. Based on my experience leading 230 teams and others' research, teams should be a maximum of 8 to 9 people (with subgroups made of 2 to 3 people each).

Third, remember that collaborating toward innovation in The 3-4-5 Method™ has proven to build a bond like no other and, therefore, can be a fantastic way to reinvigorate relationships and demonstrate dedication to honing collaboration and innovative capabilities. Therefore, in making your selections, I urge you to consider the journey as an opportunity to strengthen an existing bond or capitalize on a potential new relationship between professionals from across your organization (i.e., from different departments' offices, practice groups, business units, or geographic locations) *and* external or internal clients.

In addition, think about participant selection as an investment in future leadership, that is, select individuals who you believe will be adaptive leaders of the future. In choosing individuals, look to those who have leadership and business development potential and could benefit from the additional skill building that comes from the Method. Ideal candidates include those who are about to be or were just appointed to leadership positions. Additionally, I have found that participants who thrive on the journey possess an innovative and entrepreneurial spirit, the desire to embrace the challenges of collaboration, a zest for cross-cultural teamwork, a willingness to boldly engage in community brainstorming, the ability to creatively solve problems, demonstrated leadership qualities, and a proven strong work ethic. This is why I emphasize the importance of saying "yes" to the "eager beavers" (as opposed to focusing on trying to convince the "naysayer Debbie downers"). Also, consider hosting a competition for participation. For example, I ran an internal innovation journey program at Microsoft for 5 years, and we always had to shut down the application process within a week because we were over-inundated. Similarly, Unilever created an internal competition to join a team on a 4-month journey in LawWithoutWalls. Four hundred prospective participants were invited to submit in 350 words or less why they should be chosen to participate. And guess what? Two hundred of the 400 professional service providers applied. Figure 2.2 shows the winning entry, designed as a box. How creative is that?

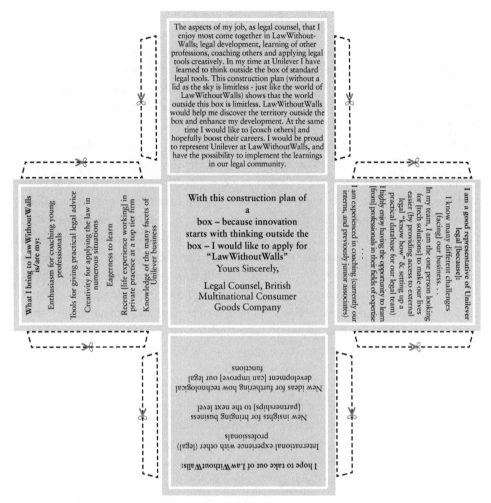

Figure 2.2 Unilever's **internal** competition winning entry.

Alternatively, you could ask participants to create a 2- to 3-minute video (via phone, tablet, computer, camera, or animated tools like Powtoon) that includes examples of their problem solving, leadership, and creativity skills and that answers a set of questions such as those below:

- How would you define innovation in 15 seconds or less?
- What was your dream job as a child, and why?
- How would you deal, or how have you dealt in the past, with a difficult teammate or coworker?
- What is the hardest thing you have ever done professionally or academically?
- How have you creatively solved a problem in the past?
- Why do you want to participate on this innovation journey?

Now, it is also true that in LawWithoutWalls we do not ask only what can the participant bring to LawWithoutWalls, but also what can LawWithoutWalls bring to the participant? So also keep an open mind that, in addition to the eager beavers, you might also want to select some people as participators who are high-potential, but who need to hone some more of the collaborative problem finding and solving skills/attributes in the Skills Delta.

Likely the most important note about participation selection deserves repeating: INCLUDE CLIENTS on the journey—and not as an afterthought. Reach out to them early in this process and seek their input, especially on the topic challenges. Invite them to participate on the team in one of the identified roles. Or consider: Could the head of marketing at one of your clients' organizations serve as a marketing or business planning or pitching expert? Could the CEO participate as a judge at the ConPosium? And absolutely include them if the topics relate to your clients' industry or services you provide them. One of the worst client service stories I ever heard was how upset a client was because their firm came to them beaming with pride to say that they had just held a weekend hackathon to hack on this client's challenges. The client was so mad that they hadn't even included the client in any way in the picking of the topics or the hacking. Talk about the opposite of client centric! And, by the way, one of the reasons LawWithoutWalls has been so successful is that sponsors almost always include internal or external clients on their teams. In fact, the Unilever competition above was for participation on a team that was sponsored by a firm (for which Unilever was a client).

Last, and related to the above point about clients, determine who will serve as judges (and experts if you are including them on the journey)—and include people external to the organization, not just the board or senior leaders within your firm or company. Having influential judges and experts works as an incentive to elicit participants (including clients) as well as an incentive along the way to ensure teams feel the pressure to perform on this journey (despite their "day jobs'" that pay them).

D.   IDENTIFYING TEAM PROJECT TOPICS

Approximately 1 to 2 weeks prior to the KickOff, some decisions need to be made related to the types of project topics the team(s) will be assigned and how they will be selected and assigned. In LawWithoutWalls, each team is assigned a *topic challenge* by its sponsor (or the sponsor's client). The challenge represents a pain point or opportunity for the assigning entity. Generally, the person or committee that picks the challenge is very senior. For example, when I ran the LawWithoutWalls-like program at Microsoft, the challenges were selected by the nine people who directly reported to Microsoft President, Brad Smith, based on the strategic growth areas that Brad Smith had prioritized as important. The challenge can focus on anything that is of importance to the entity. It could be about increasing business: *How can a payment provider, like Visa, collaborate with tech startups to navigate regulations and drive industry transformation?* Or it could be about improving the efficiency of the department: *How can professional service providers use technology to enhance their value without having to invest a huge amount of money?* Or it could be about enhancing CSR (corporate social responsibility) and ESG (environment, social, and governance): *How can advances in technology further a reduction in food waste? Or facilitate faster clinical trial processes of new drugs in a way that is safe and effective?*

The list of options is endless, including enhancing the internal or external client experience, increasing efficiency internally, improving talent recruitment or development, enhancing learning and development, productizing current services, etc. Team project topics often derive from the following: internal priorities and initiatives, pain points and opportunities for growth (either internal to the department or faced by an internal or external client), emerging trends and forecasted issues, or social justice and CSR/ESG.

Given how hard the narrowing process is, I believe in narrowing the topic challenge a bit for the teams before they even begin. Let's say the topic for the company or firm is to improve talent development during the pandemic. This topic might be further narrowed to one about finding ways to develop people to be better managers online. Or let's say the topic of interest is enhancing knowledge sharing between the various business professional service providers at the company or firm, for example, between the marketing and public relations department, between the audit and consulting departments, or between management consulting and legal advisory services. One could let the team narrow this topic down on their own, or they could be assigned a narrower project topic related to the specifics that spawned the idea, that is, whether it was to improve client service, competitive edge, or internal collaboration and efficiency. So, a narrower topic could be: *How can consulting firms capture, retain, access, and share more complete, accurate, and detailed ongoing matter information to help firms win more requests for proposals ("RFPs") and new business?* Or let's say a bank is trying to figure out how it can leverage distributed ledger technology to improve the interactions between banks and their clients. This is fairly broad. Again, the team *could*, during Steps 1 and 2 (defined more fully below), cast a wide net and eventually narrow it down to one area of banking and client interactions. Alternatively, more detail could be provided to narrow it for them. For example, the focus could be on streamlining and making the syndicated loan process more trustworthy and transparent.

In addition to narrowing, I'm a big fan of putting some creativity into the topic title. What this does is serve to lighten the constraint from the narrowing, that is, open the team members' minds to the idea that there is room for more narrowing and problem finding—and of course, it reemphasizes the need to bring out our crayons. For example, in the instance of the broad topic related to food waste suggested in the paragraph above: *How can advances in technology further a reduction in food waste?* That topic could be narrowed down and lightened up with: *Waste Not, Want Change: How can we provide consumers with the right data to combat food waste in the home and change food behaviors?* Or let's say the original broad topic was: *How might advancements in tech and AI be used to empower immigrant families in the United States?* This could be further narrowed down and lightened up with: *Tech for Good: How can legal technology be used to better prepare volunteers for their pro bono service endeavors so that they can hit the ground running and ensure that learnings from prior volunteers are not lost?*

A benefit to picking a topic (and a narrower) topic prior to KickOff is that this gives the Lead Facilitator the opportunity to provide some background information to the team, that is, articles to read or survey research or anecdotal evidence that further explain the problem or opportunity (but, of course, not all of it need come before KickOff!). In the example above about a bank's syndicated loan process, in addition to background reading about syndicated loans in general (what they are, how they work, how they came to be), the Lead Facilitator could provide some background information in the form of testimonials or examples that demonstrates that currently the process is messy, risky, time consuming, inefficient, and frustrating, with multiple versions of contracts in various stakeholders hands at a time. Additionally, I generally prefer that the person or group of people that picked the challenge (i.e., who care about it) personally provide some background as to why it was picked. This can be delivered via a short audio or video message or email. Since the point is to have a diverse team of participants, not only in discipline but also expertise, experience, culture, and age, providing some background to those that are *not* familiar with the topic—or who are greener than others—can help the team begin working faster and also ensure there is no confusion among the members about the topic that can stem from culture differences or differences in expertise.

However, one word of caution. Please be mindful that we do not want the topic to be so narrow that there is only one solution or only one problem within. I say this for a few reasons. First, problem finding is, of course, one of the critical skills to be learned during the journey. Second, we want the team participants to fall in love with their problems (and eventually also with their consumer target audiences). This is because a core essential experience of any type of innovation is what design thinkers like me call "inspiration," and when we are in love, we are inspired. And when we are inspired, when we have passion for something, we are moved. We are willing to put more work in. Warren Buffett, Steve Jobs, and Mark Zuckerberg all have famous quotes about following your passion. And that passion can sometimes even be born out of frustration. For example, Sir James Dyson invented the bagless vacuum cleaner because he was frustrated with the smell from the dust, the lack of power, and the loud noise of traditional vacuum cleaners.[5] Richard Branson created Virgin Airlines out of passionate frustration.[6] So passion for the problem (whether it is love-like or hate-like) is essential to getting teams through the tiring, exhausting process that comes in Step 2 around problem finding and refining. So, give the teams a topic that is not too broad but also one in which they can find a narrower problem within that they can fall in love (or hate) with.

---

[5] *See*, e.g., Shoshana Davis, *Vacuum Inventor James Dyson on Desire to "Change the World"*, CBS NEWS (Jan. 14, 2014), https://www.cbsnews.com/news/why-vacuums-sir-james-dyson-on-the-story-behind-his-invention/; Christopher Ategeka, *How to Turn Pain and Frustration into Entrepreneurial Opportunities: Key Lessons from Successful Entrepreneurs*, THRIVE, last visited July 9, 2022, https://thriveglobal.com/stories/lessons-from-successful-entrepreneurs-show-us-how-to-turn-frustration-into-entrepreneurial-opportunities/.

[6] Ryan Robinson, *Richard Branson on Finding a Business Idea: Listen to Your Frustrations*, FORBES (May 10, 2016), https://www.forbes.com/sites/ryanrobinson/2016/05/10/richard-branson-on-finding-a-business-idea-listen-to-your-frustrations/?sh=47224c0b4818.

E. CREATING TEAMS AND ASSIGNING ROLES

After topics are decided (1 to 2 weeks prior), it is important to identify and place participants on teams based not only on your goals related to diversity and enhancing relationships but also the subject matter of the topic. Sometimes it is helpful to peruse the LinkedIn backgrounds of the participants to find unknown experiences and talents that could prove helpful or are synergistic to the topics. For example, if the topic challenge is related to helping a pharmaceutical company client increase the efficiency of the clinical trial process, someone who has a background in healthcare, or who went to nursing school for a couple years, or who volunteers at a hospital might be a good fit—and this may be something you didn't even know about the person prior to visiting their LinkedIn. Another way to think of the makeup of the team (in addition to trying to be as diverse as possible in age, culture, experience, expertise, gender, and discipline) is with respect to work styles. So this is also a good time to have participants take DiSC assessments and then to map the team so that at the KickOff, they can see their strengths and their gaps as a team. Note, I am constantly tempted to create teams based, in part, on their DiSC profiles to ensure diversity in DiSC work style types. Yet, every year, I resist the urge. This is because in life and at work, we are not put on teams that have an even mix of types of professionals based on work style. And in life, and at work, adjusting and flexing to meet others' styles is imperative to successful relationships of all kinds and adaptive leadership.

After assigning people to teams, next, it is important to divide the team into subgroups and assign roles. Figure 2.3 shows a sample team set up.

The first subgroup is made up of approximately three Hackers. They are at the core of the team. They are the doers. They work alongside the Lead Hackers on every step of

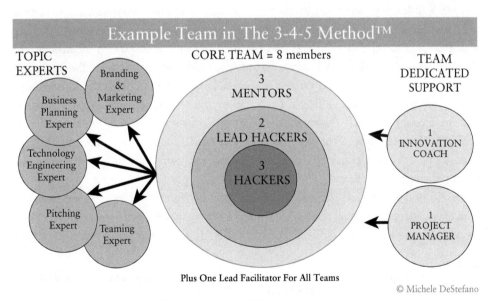

© Michele DeStefano

Figure 2.3 Example team in The 3-4-5 Method™.

the development of the project from the investigative research, problem re-finding, target audience and key stakeholder identification, idea generation, business case development, to prototype creation. They are also responsible for creating the creative work e.g., the final slide-deck and any animations or videos to bring the consumer story or solution/prototype to life that will be presented at the ConPosium. They attend all of the webinars and meetings and present on stage at ConPosium. Although the Hackers have autonomy, they work within the culture and expectations set by the Lead Hackers and also incorporate guidance, feedback, and expertise of the Mentors, Project Manager, Innovation Coach, and Lead Facilitator throughout the process. In LawWithoutWalls, the Hackers are the students but in other teams that I have facilitated, the Hackers were not less senior than the other members of the team. Ideally, however, the Hackers will have less experience and expertise in the topic assigned so that they can bring the novice or fresh perspective that is essential in creative problem solving. As Oliver Wendell Holmes aptly stated, "many ideas grow better when transplanted into another mind than in the one where they sprang up."[7]

The second subgroup is the Lead Hackers. Given their expertise and experience, Lead Hackers often have a deeper level of understanding related to the assigned problem than do the Hackers or Mentors as many will have experienced a problem within the topic or have expertise in it. They also usually have more at stake than the other members of the team. The Lead Hackers serve as team leaders. Note: we purposefully call them Lead *Hackers* as opposed to Team Leaders so that they realize they are "hacking" on the problem too. They are rolling up their sleeves and working, not just "leading." As such, they lead the team in identifying the discrete problem and its root causes and in developing creative and practical solutions to the problem identified. They provide critical feedback and commentary on the Hackers' work and teaming efforts as they progress. They attend all of the webinars, Milestone Meetings with the Lead Facilitator, and the two Innovation Coaching Sessions and are strongly encouraged (but not required) to attend the PM Meetings. They also guide the development of and lead the final dynamic presentation on stage at the ConPosium. In LawWithoutWalls, we identify the Lead Hackers as having the final say if there is disagreement in direction or if the team lacks the ability to decide by consensus or vote. Also, in LawWithoutWalls, the Lead Hackers are the participants from the sponsor and the sponsor's clients. However, this is not necessarily who should fill these roles. It can vary. However, one of the subgroups (or the Lead Facilitator or Innovation Coach) needs to be identified as having the final say in case the team cannot find consensus on a matter during the journey.

In addition to the Lead Hackers subgroup, there is one other subgroup, the Mentors, who have expertise in either the topic or in The 3-4-5 Method™ or in mentoring generally. Regardless, all Mentors are guiders. They generally use their experience and connections

---

[7] Good Reads, https://www.goodreads.com/quotes/800699-many-ideas-grow-better-when-transplanted-into-another-mind-than (last visited May 8, 2023).

to support and advise the team related to problem solving, research, *and* professional growth. We always say to our Mentors that they should treat every moment as a teaching moment and keep tabs on the teaming dynamics so that they can identify and guide the team if one participant is souring the team by, for example, railroading or bulldozing the team. As discussed in my books, the bad apple theory is alive and well. The Mentor's role is also to ask probing questions to challenge group-think and advise the team about the proposed solution to ensure that it solves the business challenge in a valuable, viable way and that there is a potential for return on investment. Mentors who have prior experience in the Method also serve as the navigators, helping the team navigate the journey and translate what feels like new words and new ways of working into tangible understanding. Mentors are invited to attend all webinars and meetings of all types that are in the calendar. Ideally, they will attend the PM meetings at least two times a month, almost all of the Milestone Meetings, and a rehearsal. However, they can add substantial value in the feedback and counsel they provide to the team by reviewing their work product between the formal meetings. Lastly, Mentors can present at ConPosium if the team needs them to, but it is not a formal part of the role.

That's the core of the team. However, we also assign a couple of people (who are external to the core but still part of the team) to help the team progress.

First, as mentioned above, each team is assigned a Project Manager, who prevents team drift. They monitor the team's progress to ensure their team is on track toward meeting its deliverables. The Project Manager helps assign tasks to ensure that teams move from problem to solution using the 5-Step method efficiently and effectively over the journey. Of course, the Lead Facilitator can play the role of Project Manager. However, when the Method is used for 3 to 4 months and there are more than a handful of teams on the journey, it can be useful to have dedicated Project Managers for each team, who have weekly (or twice monthly) meetings. And I highly recommend that you have them read this book on how to run those weekly meetings to ensure that the teams progress through the 5 Steps and meet their deadlines. Last, with respect to Project Managers, they should be made well aware of the heavy load they have. They need to understand The 3-4-5 Method™ as well as the assignments and the exercises in order to do their job, and they need to keep the team files on the selected shared platform in a logical and organized manner. Because PMs meet with the team almost every week and they attend the Milestone Meetings (led by the Lead Facilitator), they are not required to attend the webinars, the optional expert meetings, or Innovation Coach sessions. However, they are encouraged to do so because it will aid their ability to project manage the teams.

Second, each team is assigned an Innovation Coach who has experience in innovation or intrapreneurship and helps drive the team to innovate successfully. We prefer that the Innovation Coach have experience leading teams on an innovation journey so that they can cut through the haze and help the teams connect the dots that need to be connected. However, that is not always possible within organizations. In that situation, the Coach could be someone who is good at coaching vs mentoring. Coaches (as opposed to Mentors) are more performance driven. They should feel like they have a huge stake in the success of the solution. The Mentors, on the other hand, take a more holistic approach. Their role is not only to provide feedback on viability but also on teaming and personal development as well. The Coach role could be filled by an internal or external client so keep that in mind! And yes, I am repeatedly trying to convince you to include clients on the innovation journey. It's the only way to gain the MOST out of the Method. Regardless of who plays the role, the Innovation Coach holds two formal coaching sessions (Week 10 and Week 13) and is encouraged to attend the Milestone Meetings with the Lead Facilitator, and of course a rehearsal with the team. The Innovation Coach is also an ideal person to review and provide critical feedback on the script and the presentation deck prior to ConPosium.

Moreover, each team is supported by a handful of external experts in other fields necessary to the creation of a successful solution, such as branding/marketing, tech/ engineering, business planning, teaming/collaboration, and presentation/pitching. These external experts serve as advisors to multiple teams at once and are not part of any one team. Instead, they help the team by providing an external perspective based on their area of expertise. For example, the expert in pitching and presentation could watch the teams' mock rehearsals and provide critique and encouragement. The branding expert can help the team identify its brand essence and provide feedback and help on its logo and tagline and the cohesiveness and look and feel of its final presentation. The business planning expert can help with the number crunching and to ensure that a team has not left out an important piece of a business plan or failed to consider some aspect that could impact the solution's viability. This is definitely NOT to say that the branding, marketing, and tech people should be prevented from serving in one of the main team participant roles. In fact, that is a big no-no because it separates out the professionals who aren't providing the "main" service of the firm from the others and thereby creates resentment. Instead, it means that a multidisciplinary team that includes professional service providers of different backgrounds should ALSO have external support from these types of experts. Remember, if you are a branding expert and you are on a team, you are also likely to fall prey to group thinking, so having an outsider branding expert as a check in helps to prevent this.

Also, of course, there needs to be at least one Lead Facilitator. This role should be played by a leader-manager, and likely, if you are reading this book, that's you! However, because the structure of the teams is fairly flat in that decision making and accountability are pushed to all participants including the Hackers, each team requires strong leadership and close attention to each team and each project, which is why I also recommend having Project Managers for the team. Also, sometimes it is useful for the Lead Facilitator to be an expert consultant who is external to the firm or company entirely. Regardless, anyone in this role must lay out a big-picture vision while also intensely focusing on each team's 5-Step progress on technical, design, and substantive levels (while also remaining empathetic). While the Lead Facilitator should help instill a community culture that is fun, open, collaborative, and creative, they must be very transparent about the difficulty and hard work involved in the innovation journey and the expectations of each member to live up to their role, responsibilities, and culture. In other words, the Lead Facilitator, like any leader-manager, sometimes has to be a Big Bird, as discussed at length in *Leader Upheaval*. As mentioned above, the Mentors will help identify any bad apples and try to guide new behavior, but if the bad behavior persists, it is the Lead Facilitator's role to be a Big Bird and remove the person or otherwise fix the situation.

Take note, even if you truly want to be the Lead Facilitator for the journey, you still might want to consider hiring an external person to at least help you lead the KickOff event itself. An external person can sometimes more easily rein in the bad actors—and set the right behaviors—at the get-go. This is because the stakes are lower for the external person than for someone internal. Recently, I was rehired by a firm to lead a new cohort of 10 teams on an innovation journey over 3 months. (I had led some teams for this firm the year prior as well.) In the first year, we had a proper virtual KickOff and I facilitated it and trained everyone on the Three Rules of Engagement and conducted teaming and expectation setting exercises, as outlined in Chapter 3. This year, they wanted to do an in-person KickOff, but I had a prior commitment for the date of the retreat. So, the firm decided to run the KickOff on their own. Unfortunately, it went a bit awry, with some participants taking over and talking too much (like they always do when they are in committee meetings) and very little was accomplished (and the people that couldn't get a word in edgewise were annoyed). Having an external person help in the initial stages to ensure that the space and place and rules of engagement are right can make a lot of difference if you don't have the internal resources that can manage the group's tendencies to revert to old ways of working and communicating.

In a 4-month journey with lots of teams, it might also be helpful to have someone serve not just as a Teaming and Collaboration Expert but in the official capacity of External Teaming Coach—who is trained in teaming and collaboration coaching. This person works with all teams to promote individual emotional intelligence and a collective, cohesive, healthy group-working dynamic. They serve as a resource and cultural compass for teams, especially those who suffer from dysfunction or conflict. This person can actually help prevent the need for the Lead Facilitator to play the role of the Big Bird. And believe me, no matter the makeup of the teams, whether they have students on them, a mix of junior and senior professionals, or all seniors, approximately one to two teams out of every 15 teams will have a moment where a teaming coach could really help manage team dysfunction.

Of course, there are other ways to structure the teams and define the roles, and over the years of LawWithoutWalls and the 5 years leading a similar program internally at Microsoft, I have had success with different set ups. As mentioned, sometimes the Lead Facilitator has also served in the role of Project Manager for all the teams. Sometimes we have earmarked a different subgroup of mentors as alumni advisors for those who have participated in The 3-4-5 Method™ in the past. And sometimes it is not necessary to signify who

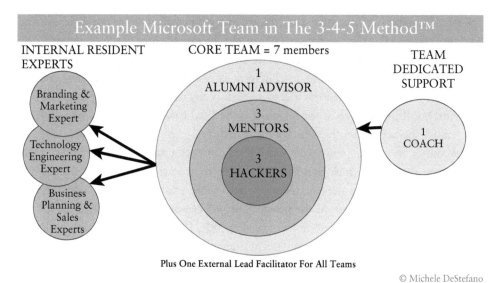

Figure 2.4 Example Microsoft team in The 3-4-5 Method™.

are the "Lead Hackers" vs the main-doer Hackers. See Figure 2.4, which represents how we set up the teams with Microsoft.

Although putting the Hackers at the center clearly delineates the Hackers as doers and having the main thrust of the work, you will note that there is no delineation as to who is "leading" the Hackers. This can be a useful way to eliminate some of the hierarchical triggers.

Also, there can be some stratification among the groups. For example, at Microsoft, we always ensured one Mentor was a topic expert on the challenge assigned and could enhance the team's understanding of the nuances of the topic and identify resources that could help the team gain the necessary industry knowledge. The topic expert Mentor differed slightly from the other Mentors because their knowledge directly enabled them to better advise the team about the proposed solution to ensure that it solves the business challenge in a valuable and viable way. Also, at Microsoft, we didn't have a Project Manager for every team. Instead, we placed an Alumni Advisor on each team, someone who had participated in the experiential learning program and worked through The 3-4-5 Method™ before. They served in a quasi-project manager and advisory role. Also, the Coach for each of the Microsoft teams was not a professional who was an expert in innovation. Instead, it was a direct report of Microsoft president Brad Smith who was in charge of this challenge and had real responsibility to find a solution that Brad Smith would support. They provided coaching two times through the journey (like the Innovation Coach does described above). However, their coaching was likely more like that of the Lead Hackers discussed above because they often had a deeper understanding of the assigned Topic Challenge than the Hackers or Mentors and a lot at stake.

The key is to modulate the roles to fit your organizational structure, naming nomenclature, the number of participants, and the length of the journey you are leading. The good news is that this team structure can be modulated to any organization, including those that are nonprofits and do not have large budgets. In the case of the latter, consider relying on people external to the organization to serve in the Coach and External Expert roles. You'd be surprised how many people are willing to volunteer and are seeking to be involved with innovation projects about changing professional services. And given that those roles are a minimum time commitment and have start and end dates, many people will answer yes if asked.

F. BUILDING COMMUNITY ACROSS THE TEAMS

As mentioned in Chapter 1 and it serves repeating: no matter the length of your journey or how many teams you have, if there is more than one team involved, it is essential that there is community building across the teams as well as among each individual team. This can be hard (especially in a virtual setting), but it can be done. It takes planning, however.

As mentioned in Chapter 1, one way we build community in LawWithoutWalls is we pick an aspirational theme and a song that matches it. Prior to KickOff, we have individuals record themselves lip syncing to a segment of our KickOff theme song. Then we splice it altogether and we play it at the beginning of the KickOff and everyone loves it. (We also play it at the ConPosium and people love it even more because they now know each other and the clips can be put into context.) In years past we have instead done a community dance move. Either way, this takes a lot of planning. Someone needs to divide the song into 15-second clips and then send an email describing what we are trying to do and convince participants to submit their video lip syncing to their assigned 15 seconds. You will likely never reach 100% participation in this, but if you decide to do a new lip sync for ConPosium, everyone who failed to participate in the first go-round will the second chance they get because now that they have seen the lip sync and met their teams, they don't want to be left out! And as mentioned in the prior chapter, when people sing and dance together, they bond. We also build community through community exercises that facilitate participants interacting with participants that are not on their teams.

And, as mentioned, we build community with Shadow Teams. Presumably, you have already had the participants take their DiSC assessment (or other workstyle assessment). After mapping each team, you can match Shadow Teams to each other based on the gaps within the teams. The goal is for the Shadow Team to fill in some of the gaps (i.e., to have some of the personality/work style types that are missing on the other team).

Another way we build community prior to the KickOff is that we host LawWithoutWalls PopUps in different places around the world to create glocal (i.e., both local and global) pockets of community. PopUps are short community and skills building events designed to help introduce LawWithoutWalls to newcomers and provide refreshers to those who have participated in LawWithoutWalls before. Hosted at various places around the world, these PopUps vary in content and form; however, each PopUp includes an interactive exercise related to teaming or creative, collaborative problem solving that attendees can later utilize in their own teaming efforts at the organizations in which they work. Also, even if your community is too small at first for a PopUp, often innovation initiatives continue on and with different cohorts over time. A PopUp is also a way to keep the community alive and prior members involved, even after they have finished their journey.

Before turning to the next chapter, which provides a roadmap for organizing and running the KickOff, you might want to take a look at Chapter 5. Remember there is prep work for the ConPosium that needs to be considered in advance of the journey. If your ConPosium is going to be virtual, then most of the prep explained in Chapter 5 can be done much later on. However, if your ConPosium is in-person and it involves many teams and a large audience, then this prep work is essential to take care of earlier on, as opposed to later.

CHAPTER **3**

Phase 1: The KickOff

The last chapter was all about the prep before the journey begins. Now we move to running and facilitating the KickOff itself, which marks the first week of the 4-month (16-week) journey.

For any meeting that involves multidisciplinary teaming (in-person or virtual), but especially for the KickOff, I recommend creating what, in LawWithoutWalls, we call a "run-of-show" that delineates content, timing, and length—to the minute—and also who will handle each task. (For a general 8-hour KickOff run-of-show, see Figure 3.1.) Having such a detailed plan ensures that the KickOff is run on time which, as talked about in great detail in *Leader Upheaval*, is essential to building trust. The run-of-show also delineates what music will be played during transitions and thinking-silent working time. And yes, I'm a big believer in using music to aid both in-person and virtual KickOffs, especially the transition to virtual breakout rooms. Music can smooth those awkward moments when people are in limbo between the main room and the breakout. Music can also help facilitate solitary thinking time while people are together in a real room or in a virtual room (with their cameras on of course). And as mentioned in the prep section in Chapter 2 when we discussed place and space, music can also help meld the community into a feeling of oneness.

Whether you are leading a 4-month, 4-week, or 3-day journey, it is important to decide up front how long your KickOff will be (to ensure you pick the right space) and because only then can you determine the length for each of the tasks/exercises. Given that the length will vary, below I provide a description of a run-of-show that works for a 1-day KickOff without delineating times. It is designed to meet the main goals of the KickOff. However, keep in mind a couple of other things.

First, although the KickOff should be planned to the minute, plan for the unplanned. Just like with any event, things go wrong. WiFi fails. PowerPoint decks become corrupted. Speakers take longer than desired. People get sick or don't show up due to professional obligations (especially client needs). Second, include diverse voices as the presenters and facilitators at the KickOff. I learned this the hard way. After a 1-day Kick-Off in Spain, I received the feedback that it was phenomenal that we had mostly female

The 3-4-5 Method™: 8-Hour KickOff General Run-Of-Show

HOUR	CONTENT
1	Starting with Why and a Teaming Icebreaker
2	Introducing and Practicing the Three Rules of Engagement
	Break
3	Setting Expectations and Explaining the 3-4-5 Method™
4	Creating Team Identity and Understanding Work Styles
5	Lunch
6	Exploring the Talent and Topic
7	Creating P.A.C.T.s and Reviewing Upcoming Deliverables
8	Cocktails or Dinner: Celebrating The First Small Wins

© Michele DeStefano

Figure 3.1 8-Hour KickOff General Run-of-Show.

presenters and that they were also ethnically diverse. Indeed, we had five presenters in total. Four of them were female presenters (two Caucasian, one Asian, and one African American) and the fifth was a white male. But then the person said, "but I really wish there was more of a mix of accents. That American accent all day long can be very tiring." He had me on that. The four females were all American and only the white male was not. He was British. The overall participant mix at Sprint as it relates to countries lived in was approximately 20% American, 30% European Union (including Denmark, France, Luxembourg, Lithuania, Germany, Netherlands, Poland, Spain), 30% United Kingdom, 20% mix of South and Central American (including Argentina, Chile, Mexico, Peru) and people from Australia, Canada, India, Pakistan, South Africa, Switzerland, and Turkey. So, try to have a diverse representation of those who are participating AND those who are leading the event.

Third, in addition to always, *always* opening up with the why—why everyone is attending the KickOff—it is important to stress that we are NOT attending the KickOff in order to solutionize—that is not one of our "whys." As discussed in great detail in my other books, professional service providers excel at complex problem solving and are incentivized by it. Therefore, many of them rush to solve and, as a result, sometimes solve for symptoms instead of root causes. So be warned: many of your participants might be wanting to jump in and solve the challenges that were assigned. Indeed, they may have shown up with solutions already. Nip this in the bud right away. Explain the importance of problem finding and hammer home that NO solutionizing will take place, nor be allowed.

To that end, an ideal run-of-show for an 8-hour, 1-day KickOff is as follows.

A. STARTING WITH WHY AND A TEAMING ICEBREAKER

First, as mentioned before, I always, always open up with the why—why we are attending the KickOff and why we are going on an innovation journey. I generally introduce Simon Sinek's book *Start with Why*[1] to make the point that the most successful companies, like Google, Apple, Amazon, Facebook, and Microsoft start with why they do what they do, not *what* products they create or services they provide. And the WHY for the KickOff is as follows:

1. To learn about The 3-4-5 Method™ and dip our toes into Step 1 of the 5 Steps.
2. To develop an inclusive culture of collaboration and innovation and commit to and practice the Three Rules of Engagement (i.e., the best ways to team and collaborate in a multicultural, multigenerational diverse team.)
3. To get to know teammates personally and professionally and to create a team identity.
4. To identify and commit to individual and team goals, protocols, and expectations.

After homing in on these larger "whys," I like to introduce a couple of key leaders who are supporting the journey and who can emphasize the reasons why the journey is so important. Generally, I have the key leaders speak not only about the challenges facing the participants and the solutions they will eventually come to, but also about the skills they develop along the way. Having a person other than me talk about the benefit of using The 3-4-5 Method™ and going on the journey helps participants absorb this information better than if it only came from me.

I also like to have the key leaders deliver their talk in the same format and timing as the final presentation will be delivered. As you already know, I'm a big fan of Ignite-style presentations (5 minutes, 20 self-advancing slides), so I like to have these presenters deliver Ignite presentations about why the Method works and what to expect. However, if you are presenting in a different style, that's fine. The point is to showcase the format you choose to ensure that everyone knows what type of presentation they are expected to give and demonstrate its difficulty and that it requires stage presence and collaboration. Doing this is like a BOGO (buy-one-get-one-free) because the presenters explain the benefits AND also showcase the type of presentations that will be required by each team at the end during the ConPosium.

After the intro of "why," it's time to move to a short, icebreaker-like team building exercise. I like to do a *Start with Why Exercise* that asks people to share why they individually are on this journey and not only what they hope to accomplish but also what skills they want to hone. (I also use this exercise to teach better networking, i.e., when someone asks you what you do, do not give them a title or generic overview. Instead, answer with

---

[1] Simon Sinek, Start with Why: How Great Leaders Inspire Everyone to Take Action (2009).

why you do what you do. It makes the conversation so much more engaging and memorable.) Combined with this, I like to conduct a *Delta-Skills Vision Exercise*. I ask each person to reflect on which two skills or attributes on the Professional Skills Delta they believe they are really good at and that they are willing to bring better over the 4-month journey. I explain that we all get rusty over time (perhaps when we were first promoted, we spent a lot of time learning about how to give feedback but lately have forgotten to use that skill) or we forget to utilize our natural talents or strengths—sometimes they are ones we use at home all the time but fail to bring to work (or vice versa). So, I ask people to pick two they can commit to bringing to their team and to bring them even better than usual. Then I ask people to reflect on which two they really should (or want to) strengthen or hone over the next 4 months.

I like to conduct this exercise with visuals. For example, I usually have two triangles drawn on two different sheets of easel paper, one labeled "Skills/Attributes We Will Bring Better" and one labeled "Skills/Attributes We Want to Hone." Then I ask the participants to write the two skills/attributes they want to bring on two different Post-it® notes (with their initials) and place them in the correct section on the Delta. Then I ask them to do the same for the skills/attributes they want to hone. It is really interesting visually to see where the Post-its® fall. I find most often they fall in the middle of the Delta (involving collaborative, creative problem finding and solving skills/attributes) but sometimes also in the bottom part of the Delta housing the C.O.S.T. skills (i.e., those skills that are concrete, related to the organization in which the person and their client works, service oriented, and involving technology). See Figure 1.1. I have the teams take pictures so they remember. Then, we have the participants explain to their teams which skills are their strengths and which they want to improve upon. As discussed in *Leader Upheaval*, by saying their strengths out loud, they feel appreciated and that they can contribute. By saying their weaknesses out loud, they are more likely to commit to shoring them up! (Note: if you are conducting a virtual KickOff, this can easily be done by pre-creating the Deltas on Google Jamboards (a collaborative whiteboard). Then people place virtual Post-its® on the Deltas.

B.   INTRODUCING AND PRACTICING THE THREE RULES OF ENGAGEMENT

After the first initial team building exercise, let participants know (i.e., warn them) that the better part of the day will be spent on teaming exercises. This may make participants uncomfortable but as Eleanor Roosevelt is famous for saying, "Do one thing every day that scares you. Those small things that make us uncomfortable help us build courage to do the work we do." Yet these teaming exercises help us start to fill in the gaps. I like to introduce the Three Rules of Engagement at this point, that is, the rules that we, as a community, are committed to following to ensure we create a collaborative, safe, inclusive environment. As discussed at great length in my prior books, the Three Rules of Engagement that I believe are essential are having an Open Mind, Open Heart, and Open Door.

Given that this is a handbook that assumes you have read *Leader Upheaval* or *Legal Upheaval*, extensive detail will not be provided on each rule. However, I will point out a few things.

First, these rules are not religious—even if they sound like it, they are different from any versions you have seen that are related to churches! Second, these rules may sound corny on their face but I have witnessed them changing lives. Seriously, people who have adopted them have told me how the rules have changed how they behave at home and at work and that, importantly, they change how others behave towards them. This is because they enter teaming and collaboration initiatives with new mindsets, with an Open Mind. They let go of preconceptions and hierarchies. They understand that we project similarity upon others when actually we are all different. And they listen with an inclusive, growth mindset, one that understands that we have to build on each other's ideas and say "yes and" instead of "no" and "but." They learn to listen with an Open Heart and they explore the true meaning of empathy and practice it—even when it's hard—understanding that helping isn't fixing, and that an empathetic response never begins with a silver lining statement that begins with. "Well, at least . . ." They learn that an empathetic response does not attempt to show the person all that they have because that person first needs to mourn that which they do not. And, perhaps most importantly, they keep an Open Door—understanding the importance of diversity and that diverse viewpoints are the key to innovation and creative, complex problem solving.

And the best way to make sure that people don't roll their eyes when you introduce the Three Rules of Engagement is to have live testimony from former participants who can give examples of how following them has helped them build and transform long-lasting relationships with others—especially clients.

Of course, you can create your own rules of engagement. *Either way, make the expectations of collaborative behavior clear.* Then have the teams practice the rules of engagement in another teaming exercise.

Preferably this exercise is one that includes the whole community and some mixing up of the community so that people can meet others on the journey who might not be on their team. I have used many different exercises to do this, including a *Find Your Partner Exercise* that requires people to find their matching pair, like Batman and Robin or Mickey and Minnie Mouse, and I have also made up my own including one that I call the *Silver and Gold Exercise*, that leverages the old children's nursery rhyme adage: *Make New Friends but Keep the Old, One Is Silver and the Other Gold.*

Then, it is likely time for a break!

C.   SETTING EXPECTATIONS AND EXPLAINING THE 3-4-5 METHOD™

After the break is a great time to explain what a Project of Worth is; the methodology of The 3-4-5 Method™, including the 5 Steps; what is special about the Method; and then share a gold standard example, that is, share a real prior topic challenge, the narrower problem, and the solution brought to life, along with the commercial the team created and the consumer stories. Be very clear what each team is required to do, that is, that they were each assigned a topic challenge and that their charge is to move from a broad to a narrow problem for a discrete target audience, create a viable solution (prototype and business plan) with a brand name and tagline and commercial—and then deliver all of that in an Ignite presentation (or another expected format) to a large audience and some expert judges who will ask questions and provide feedback at the ConPosium.

Depending on the length of the KickOff, we do one of two things to teach and prepare them for the Method. If it is a shorter KickOff, that is, one day or less, we show them how a team progressed through the 5 Steps and have a team present their final Project of Worth like they did at ConPosium, so the bar is set high. If it is a longer KickOff, we do the former PLUS we have each of the teams do a fast run-through of the Method. We assign them a "fake" challenge that is accessible to all (e.g., *How Can We Improve Higher Education?*) and have them practice the same exercises they will do later "for real" to move through the 5 Steps. We even have them do a minipresentation like that which will be expected at the ConPosium.

In sum, in a one-day KickOff, we generally do not have time to assign teams to do a "practice" challenge to practice the exercises they will do later "for real" to move through the 5 Steps. Instead, we show them what is the right end result via demonstrations and presentations.

After you have shown what the end result needs to be, and the deliverables along the way, then it is important to go into detail about the structure of the teams and sub-groups and expectations for each role, as described in Chapter 2.

D.   CREATING TEAM IDENTITY AND UNDERSTANDING WORK STYLES

Now that you have scared them a little, it is a good time to move to another teaming exercise. This is because they now really "get" why they need to congeal and become cohesive and practice the rules of engagement preferably in a teaming exercise. Whatever exercise you use, it should preferably be a little bit silly and also help the teams create a team name and identity. It's even better if it enables the team to share their work style preferences and negotiate roles and tasks with each other (which mirrors what they will have to do on this innovation journey). In *Leader Upheaval*, I describe a few exercise options like *The Restaurant*, but there are others like *The Zoo*, *The Band*, and

La Tienda that meet these goals (all of which can be accessed on my websites). Oh, and don't forget to mention (or mention again) the *why*, that is, the importance of taking the time to team and why team identity names/bonds work and are memorable; they break down cultural and hierarchical barriers given the element of "play."

Since the teams have gotten to know each other personally by this point, it is time to learn about each other's work styles and preferences. As mentioned earlier in KickOff prep, I'm a big fan of teams taking some type of professional work style test (like DiSC) and mapping the individuals on a team map (prior to KickOff) so that at KickOff the teams can (apply their new-found self-knowledge in teaming exercises like those mentioned above and) discuss their strengths and weaknesses openly. To that end, I like to have an expert in whatever work-style tool we have used to present at KickOff and then lead a role-playing exercise to enhance understanding of the different styles (including adaptive and natural) and practice flexing to engage better with others who are of a different style. However, if you can't find an expert to do this, I have also had teams do an exercise I made up called *The Bittersweet Workstyle Exercise* which is about sharing what participants learned when they read the results that might have felt a little negative, that is, that they might feel sort of bitter about and also what was sort of sweet to find out about their strengths. It concludes with *The Filling in the Team Holes Exercise*, which asks participants to look at their team map and discuss the strengths of the team but also the holes they discover; what are the work-style gaps, what's missing and, importantly, who might be willing to stretch and flex to fill those gaps.

Now it's time to let the group have organic connection time together over lunch.

E.   EXPLORING STEP 1, THE TALENT, AND THE TOPIC

After lunch is a great time to have the teams dip their toes into some substance with an overview of Step 1 and then some kind of *Talent and Topic Expertise Exploration Exercise*. By this time, the participants will be antsy to discuss the topic they were assigned. As discussed in more detail in *Leader Upheaval*, the purpose of this exercise is twofold. It is for each team to understand who has any ties to or experience with the topic, and, if so, what. Also, the purpose is for the team to uncover any hidden talents that might be useful. No matter how you run the exercise, the key is for it to be a knowledge harvesting and associating exercise. Be sure to explain that the purpose of this exercise is for each team member to spend some time reflecting on what their topic challenge means to each of them individually and how they might add value given their experience, background, expertise, emotional, or other nonsubstantive connection to the topic. In other words, in addition to uncovering relevant expertise, the goal is for participants to discover how they might associate aspects of themselves that are unrelated to their knowledge or expertise to the topic challenge in a way that might add value. For example, if a participant's prior career was as an emergency medical technician, although this expertise may have nothing to do with the topic assigned to the team, those skills will likely prove very useful when the team is facing a deadline or conducting a SWOT analysis.

And Yes!, Another Teaming Exercise: At this point, it is smart to lighten the mood with another teaming exercise that challenges the team to apply the Three Rules of Engagement (or whatever rules of engagement you have created for your community). The exercise you choose might be *The Pet-Peeve-Motto Exercise* or it might be a quick game of *Doctor Know It All*, both of which can be found on my websites. The list is endless, but the point is the same.

F. CREATING P.A.C.T.s AND REVIEWING UPCOMING DELIVERABLES

The substantive part of the day should conclude with the teams making *P.A.C.T.s* as to their *Purpose*, individual and group *Accountability*, desired *Creative Cadence*, and *Timing*. Be sure to explain that *The P.A.C.T. Exercise* is essential for teams to be able to collaborate effectively on a go-forward. And as discussed in greater length in *Leader Upheaval*, when the team participates in the development of the purpose and discussion of who is accountable for what and how it will be decided, it not only creates clarity but inclusivity and buy-in because everyone's perspectives are acknowledged (even if not adopted). *P.A.C.T.s* take into account individual preferences and also asks individuals to make some commitments. Importantly, this is a time for both individual and team accountability to be worked out and committed to, along with teaming cadence. Teams need to agree on communication and collaboration preferences and they need to agree on a weekly time to meet as a team and where/how/when and who will be responsible for what. It's important to start by showing the full calendar and provide handouts of the *Master Planner*/Syllabus and especially be sure to explain what has to be completed before the first team meeting with the Project Manager (next week, which is week 2 of the 16-week journey). Other than finishing their *P.A.C.T.s*, generally, I don't assign much in between KickOff and the first meeting. At this point, you can describe the collaborative tech platforms and apps that will be used, but don't go into major tech training here. It is too tedious and the last thing you want is people on their devices becoming frustrated or scared that it will be too much for them to learn new ways of collaborating with each other AND new technology.

Also, it's worth reiterating that it is very important that each team picks the time and day that they will meet (as a team) weekly with the Project Manager (taking into account time zone differences of course!) and on what video conferencing tool. In fact, I highly recommend that the Project Manager send out calendar requests to everyone on the team to hold weekly meeting dates and times for the next 4 months right then and there at KickOff. Note: if someone on the team was unable to make it to the KickOff, be sure to check with them before deciding the meeting times/days/dates! In fact, we often have people video conference in on a team participant's tablet during this part of the KickOff so that the team member who could not attend, can, at least, partake in the *P.A.C.T.s* and logistic decisions. This is one of the few times I recommend a hybrid approach. I don't recommend this for the other parts of the KickOff because pulling off a hybrid meeting (with some people in-person and some online is really difficult and causes problems as discussed in Chapter 2), but you can definitely use a hybrid approach to get everyone on the same page on meeting availability.

G. CELEBRATING THE FIRST SMALL WINS

Now it is time to have some fun, a cocktail party or dinner or other evening outing to celebrate the small wins that occurred during the day. This can be unstructured but at least conclude with asking participants to reflect on their takeaways and to promise to congratulate someone or their team on at least one small win from the day.

## CHAPTER 4

Phase 2: The 5 Steps to a Project of Worth

With the KickOff over, you might be wondering: now what do I do? What you should definitely NOT do is just leave it to the teams to do their work. They need weekly guidance, and this weekly guidance does not need to be done by you. Instead, as mentioned in the prep section, I recommend each team have a Project Manager that meets with the team weekly. You, on the other hand, as the Lead Facilitator, should plan on meeting with the teams five times for the 5-Step Milestone Meetings prior to the ConPosium. Below I have included instructions for each week including for the team meetings led by the Project Manager, the Milestone Meetings led by the Lead Facilitator, and rehearsals. Note: The weekly team meetings with the Project Manager ("PM Team Meetings") are *in addition* to the work the participants need to be doing within their subgroups. Thus, some might decide to hold PM Team Meetings every other week instead of every week. If you do that, then you need to cover the 2 weeks of work required in the schedule during one PM Team Meeting, which may mean you set aside 90 minutes for these PM Team meetings instead of 60 minutes.

Remember, the point of the PM Team Meetings is for the PM to provide critical feedback and to conduct exercises to move the team forward. Most of the materials should be created and reviewed prior to the team meetings so that the meetings are superefficient and effective and not filled with reports out to each other. I can't tell you what a waste of time it is for teams to create presentations to show to each other at the team meetings. These should be shared prior so that the team can discuss, receive and critique and move forward. Also, the materials shared in advance do not need to be perfect or even written. Teams can share audio recordings as well. That said, for the Milestone Meetings, I lean toward having the teams present a deck for 10 minutes or less. I do that because it puts pressure on the teams, that is, they have a real deliverable, and it is practice in co-presenting and it helps hone participants' succinct communication and collaborative presentation skills.

Figure 4.1 is a weekly calendar of a 4-month journey utilizing The 3-4-5 Method™ in list form. It mirrors the calendar shared in timeline form in Chapter 2 (see Figure 2.1). To be

WK	CONTENT AND MEETING TYPE(S)
	PHASE 1: KICKOFF (INDIVIDUAL, TEAM, AND COMMUNITY BUILDING)
1	KickOff (with a Dash of Step 1)
	PHASE 2: TEAMING THROUGH THE 5 STEPS TO A PROJECT OF WORTH
2	Webinar 1: Giving and Receiving Feedback and More Training on the 3-4-5 Method™ PM Team Meeting (Step 1)
3	PM Team Meeting (Step 2)
4	Webinar 2: Problem Finding and Refining PM Team Meeting (Step 2 with a Dash of Step 3)
5	*Milestone Meeting 1 (Steps 1–2 with a Dash of Step 3) with Lead Facilitator and PM*
6	Webinar 3: Constructing, Scripting, and Relaying Consumer Stories PM Team Meeting (Step 3)
7	*Milestone Meeting 2 (Steps 2–3 with a Dash of Step 1) with Lead Facilitator and PM*
8	PM Team Meeting (Step 4 with a Dash of Step 5)
9	Webinar 4: Prototyping Shadow Team Meeting 1 *Milestone Meeting 3 (Steps 1–4 with a Dash of Step 5) with Lead Facilitator and PM*
10	Webinar 5: Developing a Business Plan Coach Session 1 (Steps 1–5) (in lieu of PM Team Meeting This week) Optional Business Planning or Pitching Expert Meeting
11	Shadow Team Meeting 2 *Milestone Meeting 4 (Steps 1–5 Focusing on Steps 4–5) with Lead Facilitator and PM*
12	Webinar 6: Branding and Marketing Optional Branding or Tech Engineering Expert Meeting PM Team Meeting (Steps 4–5 focusing on the prototype, branding, and the business plan)
13	Webinar 7: Presenting, Storytelling, Scripting, and Deck Development Coach Session 2 (Steps 1–5) (in lieu of PM Team Meeting This week)
14	*Milestone Meeting 5 (Mock Presentations) with Lead Facilitator and PM*
15	Rehearsals with Coaches, PMs, and Shadow Teams
	PHASE 3: THE CONPOSIUM (PITCHING, ASSESSING, AND CELEBRATING)
16	Final Presentation Materials and Deck Due at least 24 hours Prior to ConPosium The ConPosium (Steps 1–5 and Celebration)

© Michele DeStefano

Figure 4.1 The 3-4-5 Method™: 4-Month Journey Weekly Calendar.

clear, this chart only delineates the essential meeting: PM Meetings, Milestone Meetings, Coach Sessions, Rehearsals, and the recommended webinars, and optional meetings with experts. It assumes that subgroups are doing the assigned work and meeting together (without the PM) regularly as needed.

As you read through the week by week descriptions below, the *Sample 4-Month Journey Master Planner*, available on my websites, can prove useful because it details the recommended deliverables and assignments by week and adds substantive materials to the overview provided below.

A.   STEP 1: EXPLORING AND INVESTIGATING THE CHALLENGE

Step 1 is about exploring and investigating the background and big picture of the challenge or topic assigned. It starts by asking questions that are open minded and inspirational. After all, we all know well that Einstein's theory of relativity began with an early beautiful question that was something like, "What if I rode a beam of light across the universe?" So starting with questions is essential. After that, the team's job is to dig in and understand everything it possibly can about the challenge assigned. Teams generally start by conducting secondary archival and bibliographical research to explore the context of the challenge, its history and regulatory environment, the demographic trends and global (or glocal) impact affecting it, the current state of the market and the technology, and statistical data they can find about the challenge and more. They do this with the goal of identifying the problems worth solving that lie within the challenge. This then helps them identify who to conduct primary research with, that is, through interviews and surveys.

Step 1 can be daunting because the assigned topics (even after some narrowing) are often thorny and broad and sometimes outside the scope of knowledge of many participants. Individuals will have different interpretations of the challenge given their varied cultures, expertise, and background. So part of Step 1 is to figure out what the challenge means to each individual on the team and also what it means in context to the team's company, department, or firm related to its purpose, values, and goals. Some of this exploration will have occurred during the *Talent and Topic Expertise Exercise* at KickOff but more needs to be done. For some participants there will be a steep learning curve. Even the language might be new, especially if the topic is one related to new tech or processes. Think AI, ChatGPT, or NFTs.

The good news is that although Step 1 begins very broad and open-ended, it eventually focuses on seeing the trees and not the forest—studying branches is something lots of professional service providers are good at. Later, however, teams will need to refocus on the forest; this can prove difficult for individuals who want to cover every aspect of a problem. Perfection in innovation is not possible at the outset of a cycle; once a narrow problem or opportunity is identified, the work lies up ahead and not behind. And once progress is made on Steps 2 and 3, there is the need to redo Step 1.

The team needs to now find secondary research (studies, data) that prove a real need exists. How many people are impacted by this problem and what are the implications (negative or positive) that have been proven by others? In other words, once a team has narrowed in on a specific problem during Step 2 of the process, returning to Step 1 is a great help in finding data to convince audiences that something needs to be done.

Generally, after a 1- or 2-day KickOff, I only spend one week on Step 1 because we began Step 1 at the KickOff and because most of the time really needs to be spent on Step 2, the narrowing of the problem. That said, understanding the big picture is essential before digging into the problem. Also, as mentioned, Step 1 needs to be revisited after a narrower problem is identified so that the team can gather the data and stats that hammer home the real need to solve this narrow problem. The overarching goals of Step 1 are to answer the following questions and more:

- What is your overarching Project Topic, that is, Topic Challenge?
- What does the Project Topic mean to you and your team?
- How do your interpretations differ given your varied cultures, expertise, and background?
- What is the history of your topic in the relevant industry, in the context of our world today in general, and in your firm/company/organization?
- How does this challenge fit into a larger context of your firm, company's, or client's business, purpose, values, and goals?
- What is the geography of the topic: Is this a global or local topic?
- What are relevant aspects of the regulatory environment, demographic trends, global impact, and state of the market?
- What are the smaller topics, problems, or opportunities that are within the assigned topic?
- What research and data exist that shows that there is a real "need" to address this challenge? Are there studies that show that a certain high percentage of people are impacted negatively by the problem and that show the positive impact that solving this problem might have?

Some of the tools and exercises to help with Step 1 include:

- *Talent and Topic Expertise Exploration Exercise* to identify and share teammates' respective expertise related to the Topic Challenge and other talents that might help the team on the journey.
- *Hal Gregersen Question Burst Exercise*[1] to uncover differences in opinion, breadth of scope, problems within the problem, causes and effects, and to unlock new ways of thinking about a challenge and an avenue of investigation that is safe for all.
- Secondary research on the internet to uncover studies and stats supporting the need.

---

[1] Hal Gregersen, *Better Brainstorming*, Harv. Bus. Rev. (Mar.-Apr. 2018), https://hbr.org/2018/03/better-brainstorming.

- Primary research by conducting interviews and/or surveys or information gathering of others in and outside your firm or company about the Topic Challenge.
- *Identifying Topic Areas of Interest Within the Topic Challenge Exercise* to identify areas within the Topic Challenge that have problems ripe for solving and that the team members care about.

Week 1: KickOff (with a Dash of Step 1)

(Described in the previous chapter.)

Week 2: Goals, Content, and PM Team Meeting Overview (Step 1)

The goals for participants for Week 2 (the week following the KickOff) are as follows. First, to gain a deeper understanding of The 3-4-5 Method™ and the 5-Step process. Second, to reflect on their roles along with their work styles and the commitments they need to honor for their team. Additionally, teams should begin to understand the general issues involved in their Topic Challenge and what the topic means to teammates, and begin the narrowing process. Last, this week is also about practicing new ways of reaching consensus and providing feedback so that when the narrowing really happens, the team can do so more easily.

In terms of content, in addition to assigned readings on cognitive bias, the art of feedback, and The 3-4-5 Method™, I recommend a webinar that provides additional training about The 3-4-5 Method™ focusing on training people on their various roles, that is, how to be a mentor or coach and also on the art of giving and receiving feedback. If you have time, you might even consider some type of diversity, inclusion, cognitive bias, and coaching training for the Mentors, Coaches, and Project Managers. We can't assume that professional service providers know how to give and receive feedback and how to appropriately deal with some of the communication challenges that multidisciplinary, multicultural, and intergenerational diverse teams pose. Even with our unbelievably warm, welcoming, open community in LawWithoutWalls, every year we have at least one complaint about a Coach or Mentor who said something that someone felt was inappropriate or culturally incompetent. This can happen regardless of training, but training can help stem this and also protect the Lead Facilitator against blame.

Given that this is the first team meeting led by the PM, it is likely best for the PM to introduce themselves and explain why they are glad to be in the PM role. Then the PM should describe their own set of expectations because each PM will have their own style. However, importantly, the PM should tell the participants that they must attend all PM Team Meetings (and with videos on). Note: I have assumed all team meetings will be held virtually given that the odds are low that the teams will be able to meet in-person if they are truly as diverse across the organization as they should be! Another must is for the PM to promise to start and end on time each week—and in our virtual world, I think all meetings that used to be an hour should now be only 50 minutes. It is too hard to zoom from one meeting to another without a breather.

Then, the PM should review the goals for the meeting and provide a roadmap, which is as follows. First, to start "right" with a teaming exercise, I recommend starting with the *Pancake or Waffles Exercise* described in *Leader Upheaval*. This is a great way for the teams to practice reaching consensus and giving or receiving feedback. Then it is time to move into Step 1. The PM should provide an overview of Step 1 to refresh people's memories of discussions at KickOff about the topic and talent. Note: the PM can use the overview of Step 1 provided above. Then, I like to start with some type of Step 1 exploration exercise like a *Hal Gregersen Question Burst Exercise* to field how individuals think about the Topic Challenge.[2]

Asking questions in a *Question Burst* is a great way to uncover differences in opinion, breadth of scope, problems within the problem, causes and effects, etc. Plus, it enables people to investigate in a safe way since everyone is required to ask questions. In a Question Burst, the group asks questions that are open-ended (not closed); short vs long (simple vs complex); descriptive (what's not working, what's working, and why); oriented to identifying the unknown; heartfelt but include a mix of positive and negative questions. And if these rules are followed, you will be amazed at how the questions inform the team of each person's perspective and focus.

A *Question Burst* also helps rule out any misunderstandings about the focus of the challenge, which is super-important on culturally diverse teams because simply one word can be misunderstood and misinterpreted. For example, one year in LawWithoutWalls, a team's challenge was: *Alternative Courts on the Brain: Psychologically Based, But How Can We Make Them Sound?* Wow, did the word "sound" cause confusion for people whose first language was not English. Confusion was doubled for those who were from countries that didn't have "alternative courts" (also sometimes called problem-solving courts). The reality is just as names matter (as discussed in *Leader Upheaval*) so do words—and given accents, even accurate words can be misunderstood. I have a quaint story that exemplifies this in a very simplistic way. When my youngest son was around seven years old, I took him with me to the car dealership to buy a car. The car salesman explained at the beginning of the meeting that he was new to the job because he used to be a "trader," that is, he meant, but didn't say, he was a *stock* trader. My son, Trip, who was sitting on my lap at the time, started getting agitated and kept trying to interrupt our negotiations. (For those of you who do not live in the United States, buying a car can be a long ordeal and can entail a lot of haggling, negotiating, and waiting . . . and waiting). I kept saying "Shh shhh," and Trip became more and more distressed. Finally, the car salesman stood up to go talk to his superior about some request I had made and Trip said loudly and pointedly: "Mom, Mom, you absolutely can't buy a car from this guy!" I looked at him, surprised, and asked, "Why not?" and he said, "Because he's a *traitor*. He even said so!" Likely this misunderstanding was because he was too young to have been exposed to what a "trader" is (though old enough to have been exposed to what a "traitor" is) but it could also have been a matter

---

[2] HAL B. GREGERSEN, QUESTIONS ARE THE ANSWERS: A BREAKTHROUGH APPROACH TO YOUR MOST VEXING PROBLEMS AT WORK AND IN LIFE (2018).

of pronunciation or labeling. Just think, in some countries the word "collaborator" is a negative one. The same is true for the word "hack" which entrepreneurs use all the time, that is, "hackathons." The point is that in giving license to everyone to ask questions—any questions—without shame or laughter and without judgment, we weed out misunderstandings and we enhance inclusivity!

When I conduct this exercise, I urge each participant to ask three different types of questions: why, how, and what. However, please understand and the PM should make the following clear to the team: **We are not yet trying to find *the* narrow problem at this point. We are trying to think big and probe the scope of the topic/challenge/ opportunity to uncover all the thorns and branches.** This exercise (combined with the discussion at the KickOff) will likely demonstrate some pockets within the Topic Challenge that need further exploration. **See the following chart that retraces the footsteps of a team sponsored by Pinsent Masons that went on a 3-4-5 Journey in LawWithoutWalls and conducted a *Question Burst*.**

RETRACING FOOTSTEPS: SAMPLE *QUESTION BURST EXERCISE*

Step 1: Exploring and Investigating the Challenge

Example Topic Challenge: Cogito Ergo Sum: *How can cognitive technologies transform the way financial institutions deal with the impact of regulatory change on their consumer lending documentation?*

- Why are we always reactive vs proactive?
- How can we predict regulatory change earlier?
- Why aren't there more ways to prove that we complied with lending requirements?
- How might we identify the impact that regulatory change will have on our lending processes before they happen?
- How might we advantageously impact regulations related to customer lending?
- What are common complaints lodged by UK consumers against banks?
- How are complaints between customers and banks handled?
- To whom are banks beholden?
- What is the role of the Ombudsman?
- What cognitive technologies do other banks use to deal with regulatory change?

The PM should record the questions from the *Question Burst* in a shared document, for example, a Google Doc, in the team folder while it is occurring.

After this exercise, the team needs to work together to create a roadmap of tasks for each member to do to further investigate the Challenge as dictated by Step 1. This could consist of secondary research or investigative interviews with the purpose to better understand the Topic Challenge and begin narrowing. So, in the example above, the questions make clear that more research needs to be done to find out about the types of complaints that are lodged, how complaints are handled by the bank, the role of the Ombudsman, and what regulations need to be addressed during the consumer lending process (and how they have changed recently if at all). Research on cognitive technologies is also critical. Some of this research could be found on the internet. Some likely could be found internally in files at the bank. Perhaps some information might need to be retrieved via meetings with some of the key players at the bank. In terms of identifying who should do what, the team's Lead Hackers and Mentors should help connect the Hackers with people to talk with and provide resources to read or watch. The Hackers should do the research and record their findings in the shared folder.

Toward the end of the meeting, the PM should review the deliverables (tasks and assignments) for the upcoming week (i.e., to be completed before the next PM Team Meeting). Don't forget to also review the tech they will be using, that is, where teams should store files and what channels are to be used for chats (Teams or Google Drive or Slack, etc.).

Last, it might be good to end the meeting with a *Quick Mood Check Exercise*. To do this, I ask participants to share their mood right now by a thumbs up (great, enthusiastic), hand flat (here, but not feeling over the top ecstatic), two thumbs down (confused and under-excited). If there are thumbs down, explore it or ask that person if they can meet later to discuss more.

B.   STEP 2: FINDING AND REFINING THE PROBLEM OR OPPORTUNITY

In Step 2, teams have to whittle down the large challenge they were assigned to a smaller, narrower problem impacting a discrete audience. There might be a primary audience and a secondary audience or two equally targeted audiences (not to mention other key stakeholders). These audiences will be further defined in Step 3—as such, there may be back and forth movement between Steps 2 and 3. Because in Step 2 the goal is identifying the narrow problem, this also means there is some back and forth with Step 1 to determine the context or history behind the narrower problem or opportunity and the stats and data supporting the narrower problem's heft and impact. This is done again with secondary research and by conducting interviews of the relevant group of people to uncover problems related to the topic. The goal is for teams to literally fall in love with their narrower problem. If they do not feel passionate about solving it, they won't. In addition, it is important that the team accurately frames the problem and separates out the true root causes of the problem from the symptoms. This is why Step 2 often turns out to be the hardest of all the steps because problem finding and framing is really hard and we are often fooled into thinking that a particular symptom is the problem. And if that occurs, we have to go back to the drawing board.

Step 2 also touches on Step 3 because in the process of defining the problem, the team needs to start identifying the various stakeholders impacting or influencing the identified problem. It is only, therefore, after Step 3 is concluded (and the team has also now settled on the one or two key, core target audiences for whom they are solving the problem) that Step 2 can "conclude" with a real *Problem Trip Mapping Exercise* and *Getting on the Same Problem Plane Exercise*, as described in *Leader Upheaval*. Though, even then, Step 2 is not done-done because Step 5 often requires revising the solution during Step 4, which may require returning to Step 2 to refine the problem yet again. The primary goals for Step 2 are to:

- Identify and converge upon a narrow problem/opportunity within the larger Topic Challenge.
- Revisit Step 1 and review the context/history behind the narrower problem or opportunity.
- Keep an eye on Step 3: Which audiences does this problem/opportunity most impact or resonate with?
- Visit Step 5 to make sure the problem is solvable.

Some of the tools and exercises to help with Step 2 include:

- Secondary research on the internet.
- Primary research—conducting investigative interviews to identify problems related to the Topic Challenge.
- *Narrower Problem Identification Exercise* to help guide individual team members' primary and secondary research to find and describe some narrower problems related to the problems the team converged upon earlier.
- Brainstorming with your team to mine for gaps and find narrower, solvable problems or opportunities within the Topic Challenge:
  - *I Hate It When Exercise* to uncover pain points (what's not working).
  - *I Just Wish Exercise* to uncover hopefuls (what could be better).
- *Problem Convergence: Passion and Practicability Exercise* to help teams converge on one narrow problem as a team in a way that accounts for the level of passion the team has for solving the identified problem and also the problem's solvability.
- *Getting on the Same Problem Plane Exercise* to gain consensus on the exact narrow problem the team is solving, who they are solving it for (i.e., key target audience(s)), and why solving the problem for these audiences is important.
- *Writing Problem Statements Right Exercise* to learn how to write problem statements with the right level of detail but that do not include a solution within them.
- *Problem Trip Mapping Exercise (Step 2 Focus)* to map the process in which the problem surfaces (which could be along a trajectory or timeline, or it could be an order of how something is accomplished or created), chunk the problem down into smaller parts to begin to identify who is experiencing or impacted by the problem (and when), and uncover all the various problems within the problem. (Note: this exercise is used again during after Step 3.)

- *Examples of Problem Trip Maps Resource* to provide examples of prior project trip maps so that teams understand how to create their maps and the level of detail that is required (and why Step 3 needs to be done before the trip map is truly completed).
- *The Butterfly Approach to Convergence Exercise* to get teams to converge on one problem anonymously.
- *Interviewing Tips and Sample Interview Template Resource.*

Week 3: Goals, Content, and PM Team Meeting Overview (Step 2)

This week is all about Step 2—narrowing the Topic Challenge and **identifying one to two discrete, narrow problems/challenges/opportunities within the larger Topic Challenge**. There is also a dash of Step 3 in this step because in identifying narrow problems, we also have to consider who is experiencing the problem. There might be a primary and a secondary group or two equally affected groups. Although the target audience will be further defined in Step 3, understand that there might be some back and forth between Steps 2 and 3—and also Step 1 to determine the context or history behind the narrower problem or opportunity. This is again done by conducting interviews of the relevant group of people to uncover problems related to the topic. Step 2 often turns out to be the hardest of all the steps. We are often fooled into thinking the symptom is the problem.

The main goal for participants for week 3 is to find narrower problems within the Topic Challenge and attempt to converge to one or two problems and to begin to identify stakeholders and target audiences impacted by the problem. At this point, participants likely don't really realize that Step 2 is the hardest part, that is, that finding a real, narrow problem that matters for a target audience that is not too big or not too small is actually a lot harder than solving the problem. The PM's number one job over the next few weeks is **to STOP participants from jumping to solutions.**

First, as always, the PM should take a few minutes at the beginning of the PM Team Meeting to do a short teaming exercise. Then provide a roadmap for the meeting. The PM should start by asking for a progress update limited to two minutes per person on the topic of "what are some of the problems you uncovered in your research in Step 1?"

After the progress update, the first exercise that the PM should conduct should be one that elicits lots of problems within the Topic Challenge. I like to do the exercise *I Hate It When* (or if you do not like the word "hate," you can call it *I'm so Frustrated When*). This exercise is designed to help source problems. Unlike an *I Just Wish Exercise*, the source of the problems come from a negative place, that is, from what drives us (or the target audience) bonkers—what frustrates us "beyond the beyond." As discussed, frustration is historically a source of great new business ideas.[3] Think Richard Branson.[4] He was

---

[3] *See supra* notes 5 and 6, Chapter 2 and accompanying text.

[4] Aly Walansky, *How Richard Branson Channeled This Negative Emotion into a Billion-Dollar Empire*, GOALCAST, https://www.goalcast.com/how-richard-branson-channeled-this-negative-emotion-into-a-billion-dollar-empire/, (last visited July 9, 2022).

supposed to be on a plane heading to the Virgin Islands from Puerto Rico when there was an announcement that the flight was delayed to the next day because the flight didn't have enough passengers. This frustrated Branson so he booked a chartered plane (that he couldn't afford at the time) and created a sign "Virgin Airlines, one-way Virgin Islands $39" and sold seats on the plane to the other frustrated passengers. This success led him to buy a plane, build his airline, and create the Virgin Group, which we all know has been a massive success.

Therefore, our goal with this exercise is to source the frustrations that (after a lot of exploration and refinement) can eventually be solved by coming up with a killer idea. So to conduct this exercise, the PM should explain that the goal is to come up with a list of 10–15 frustrations related to your team's Topic Challenge. These should be "real" frustrations that an individual has experienced (or has investigated and discovered) related to the problem . . . not fake or made-up or conjectured frustrations or problems. However, for those people who don't have direct experience with the Topic Challenge, role playing is a great tool. Remember to include the various perspectives (audiences/players) that are part of the team's overarching Topic Challenge.

- For example, if your team's topic is: *Paving the Path Forward: How can a large pharmaceutical company help refugee women and children more easily access health care relief (food, shelter, and consumer products) after they cross international borders?* Then, participants could source "I hate it whens" from any of the following perspectives/roles:
  - Legal department of a pharmaceutical company
  - CEO or CFO of a pharmaceutical company
  - The pharmaceutical company's head of CSR (corporate social responsibility) or ESG (environment, social, governance)
  - Refugee women and children
  - Nonprofits helping refugee women and children
  - Pharmacists
  - Drug stores
- Another example is, if your team's topic is: *Are You Feeling Me? How can law firms, in-house departments, and technology providers collaborate for better business outcomes?* Then, participants could source "I hate it whens" from any of the following perspectives/ roles:
  - In-house lawyer (e.g., the general counsel)
  - Procurement professionals
  - External (law firm) counsel

And remember, in the *I Hate It When Exercise*, this is divergent thinking time:

- Stay open to a wide range of possibilities
- No self-critique or analysis or editing your initial thoughts, reactions, etc.
- More is more, that is, the more problems listed the better

Look at the next "Retracing Footsteps" example of an *I Hate It When Exercise* **from the same team exemplified in Step 1.**

RETRACING FOOTSTEPS: SAMPLE *I HATE IT WHEN EXERCISE*

Step 2: Finding and Refining the Problem or Opportunity

Example Topic Challenge: Cogito Ergo Sum: *How can cognitive technologies transform the way financial institutions deal with the impact of regulatory change on their consumer lending documentation?*

- I hate it that we are always reactive instead of proactive when dealing with regulations related to consumer lending.
- I hate that the regulatory changes occur without us knowing and without being able to be prepared.
- I hate it that we complied with the lending requirements but we can't prove that we did.
- I hate that we have all these complaints that are not true and that the Ombudsman almost always sides with the consumer.
- I hate that even after all the explanations, consumers still don't understand what they are agreeing to.

During this exercise, the team should have been able to source 10–15 (or more) problems within their Topic Challenge. So now the challenge is to converge on two of the problems. I like to have teams do an exercise I made up called *The Problem Convergence: Passion and Practicability Exercise*, which essentially enables the team to converge onto two problems: one problem they feel most passionately about and one problem they believe is most solvable.

To that end, not all problems are solvable and not all solvable problems are worth solving. What do I mean by that? Some problems are just too big and broad to tackle at once, for example, world hunger. I am not saying finding a solution to combat world hunger is not important; quite the contrary. However, some problems are biting off more than we can chew, that is, the problem needs to be narrowed in order to be solvable—not to mention that we need to separate the source of a problem from the symptoms—which we will do later with *The 5 Whys and Root Cause Analysis Exercise*. As described in *Leader Upheaval*, when a team has suggested solving a problem that is too big, this is one of the few times that I recommend that the PM or Lead Facilitator behave like a Big Bird and swoop in and stop it. Other problems, however, are just too small, that is, they aren't experienced by enough people (or they aren't causing enough havoc) to justify taking the time to solve them. Remember: the problems that are selected should be "real" problems that a significant group of people are experiencing. Sometimes the problems the team feels most passionately about are ALSO the ones that are most solvable. This is kismet and not just a wonderful coincidence. Again, the goal of this exercise is to identify TWO problems the team is excited about and invested in solving that are practicable. And if the team struggles, try to use a consensus building tool or exercise like those mentioned earlier in this handbook, such as the *Pancakes or Waffles Exercise*.

The PM should record the two narrower problems in the team's folder.

The meeting should be concluded by reviewing the deliverables for the coming week, which include reading Steps 2 and 3, conducting both primary or secondary research of the two narrower problems identified during this PM Team Meeting, watching or attending a webinar on the art of problem finding and refining, and preparing two concrete narrow problem statements with real examples of the problems and who is experiencing the problem (or impacted by the problem) for the next PM Team Meeting. Instructions are laid out in the *Narrower Problem Identification Exercise*.

Week 4: Goals, Content, and PM Team Meeting Overview (Step 2 with a Dash of Step 3)

The goals for this week are for the participants to begin to learn how to refine problems and differentiate between symptoms and root causes of problems and to gain a better understanding of the narrow problems identified in the prior PM Team Meeting. They should also be keeping an eye on Step 3: With which audience do these problems/opportunities most resonate? During the meeting, they should learn approaches for unpacking different aspects of a problem/challenge and also learn teammates' perspectives and ideas about the narrower problems. By the end of the team meeting the team should have selected one narrow problem with which to proceed.

As mentioned in last week's description: The number one job for the PM is STILL to STOP participants from jumping to solutions. To that end, this week and next week are focused on problem finding and refining only. The PM should consider starting the meeting by explaining this. Then the PM should review the roadmap for the meeting and start with a short teaming exercise designed to elicit thoughts about the webinar on the problem finding and refining. I like to use the following *Best-Worst and What-I-Learned Exercise*: Each person says what they thought was the best part of the webinar, what they thought was the worst part of the webinar, and one thing they learned. As always, the teaming exercise should be done really quickly because it's important to get to the exercise! After that, the meeting should turn to an exercise that enables participants to learn about each other's perspectives on the narrower problems identified last week and converge onto one narrow problem.

As a review, for this PM Team Meeting, the participants were asked to individually prepare to present at least two concrete narrow problems with real examples of the problems and who is experiencing the problem via *The Narrower Problem Identification Exercise*. So the PM should begin by asking for a volunteer to go first to share one or two concrete narrow problems with real examples of the problem and who is experiencing the problem. Providing a time limit is essential so that everyone can be heard. (Note: participants should have already turned these in (or uploaded them to their team folder), so it will merely be a matter of reviewing them as a group).

The PM should be prepared for some frustration here—perhaps even lots of frustration. Often participants openly recognize and disagree on what the problems are. Worse yet, they sometimes disagree about the problems but do not even realize it! Further, even though they were told not to, often participants will come to this meeting with solutions (a big no-no at this point). Worse yet, often they don't recognize that they have included a solution (or indicated parts of the solution) in their problem identification descriptions. What do I mean by that? Here are some examples of problem statements that either include or are themselves "solutions" labeled WRONG and then a correct version labeled RIGHT:

- WRONG: Inhouse legal departments need a first pass review of third-party contracts that is fast and informative.
- RIGHT: General counsel do not have a clear understanding of what the legal department has committed to in third-party contracts and, as a result, do not know the level of risks that are outstanding stemming from third-party contracts. Further, when they seek information about third-party contracts, it takes a lot of time to access them and even time to review them.
- WRONG: How can we use data from successful podcasts today to provide an objective analysis to help new podcasters improve their content?
- RIGHT: All podcasters want to grow their audience to ensure their message is heard. The lack of quality content prevents listener engagement. New podcasters don't know how to create content in a way that is of high quality and engaging, nor do they know how to assess the quality of their own podcasts.
- WRONG: We want to help FinTech startups expand to other countries by helping them navigate and comply with the different regulations that exist.
- RIGHT: FinTech startups want to expand globally, but different regulations in different countries make this difficult. This is because FinTech startups are often run by nonlawyers who struggle with understanding regulations and legal issues and learning about them is costly and time consuming because many FinTechs don't have big legal departments or the resources to hire lawyers. Financial institutions, like Visa, want to court FinTech startups so that they get their future business (as they grow). Therefore, this is an opportunity for financial institutions because they do have the resources and expertise to provide guidance to FinTech startups on navigating the regulations.
- WRONG: How do we use hand-held, location-enabled technology to effectively enforce regulation around the use of drones by average drone users?
- RIGHT: Drone usage is regulated; the problem is that there's no compliance with the regulations and there are no ways to enforce it. For example, in Chile, to fly a drone,

you have to have a license, but half of drone pilots don't have the license and aren't concerned about getting one. This is a problem because the misuse of drones by average drone users has (and likely will continue) to cause harm to others (explain harm).

In addition to putting solutions into problem statements, teams often have trouble putting down on paper what they know and is in their head. They think they are really describing the problem, but they aren't. Here is an example of a problem statement that is too vague and assumptive:

- WRONG: How can small to medium enterprises discover when their employees are having personal legal issues so they can provide an accurate solution?
- RIGHT: When employees of small to medium enterprises (SMEs) experience personal legal issues, they miss time at work, are less effective at work, and use on-the-clock work time to deal with issues. SMEs do not realize that they lose money when their employees are experiencing personal legal issues. Therefore, they don't see the value in helping their employees deal with personal legal issues. It's a lose-lose situation.

While a person shares, the PM should record what they say and after they are done talking, provide feedback on the problem statements if they include solutions or are too broad as shown above. After everyone has had their turn, share the list that was created. And review the *Writing Problem Statements Right Exercise* with them. Have them take a stab at revising their problem statements.

Now, it's time to get the team to converge and pick ONE problem. Again use the *Problem Convergence: Passion and Practicability Exercise* for this purpose. Like earlier, each person picks one problem they feel most passionately about solving and one that they feel is most solvable. The participants do not have to pick the problems that they brought to the meeting. Instead, they should keep an Open Mind, Open Heart, and Open Door to others' identified problems. If doing this in-person or online, for example, in a Jamboard, the PM can use the *Butterfly Approach to Convergence Exercise* which helps participants stay anonymous and provides a visual display of the team's preferences. Essentially, each participant puts one sticky note next to a problem they feel most passionately about and one next to a problem they feel is solvable. The sticky notes are the wings of the butterfly. The problems that receive the most wings are the ones that the team has converged to. After this, if there is a tie, each participant should pick one problem that they most wish to work on that is *not* one of the problems that they brought with them. If convergence has still not happened, consider having the team reach out to other people outside the group to weigh in, perhaps their Innovation Coach or Shadow Team.

Now the group should brainstorm a list of the people within the firm or company—and/or outside the firm or company—who the team should seek to meet with to begin more exploration of the problem.

The meeting should conclude with an overview of the deliverables for the next week. Note, this coming week will be the most collaborative to date because the team has to create a joint *Problem Plane* statement and also a deck to present their progress to date in the next week's Milestone Meeting 1 (Steps 1–2 with a Dash of Step 3) which occurs at the same time as the usual PM Team Meeting but is held in lieu of it and led by the Lead Facilitator. However, the PM should join and, of course, the Innovation Coach should be welcomed to join as well.

The next "Retracing Footsteps" shows where a team might be by this point or where they should be by the next week.

RETRACING FOOTSTEPS: SAMPLE *PROBLEM PLANE* STATEMENT PROGRESS

Step 2: Finding and Refining the Problem or Opportunity

Example Topic Challenge: Cogito Ergo Sum: *How can cognitive technologies transform the way financial institutions deal with the impact of regulatory change on their consumer lending documentation?*

- Consumers of financial lending products in the UK who wish to file a formal complaint against a bank do so through the UK Financial Ombudsman Services. Proving compliance is complicated and difficult, requiring the bank to undergo a hefty procedure in a nonsystematic way.
  - The Ombudsman shifts the burden of proof of compliance to the bank.
  - The deadline to prove compliance tolls once any part of the bank has been notified of the complaint.
  - This often results in banks, although compliant, paying penalties to consumers over an inability to meet the burden on time.
- Complaints against banks from consumers have always happened, will continue to happen, and are increasing in frequency and cost.
- Broad categories where the problem is likely to occur include interpretation of changes in regulation, implementation of the interpreted regulation through policies, and enactment of policies in day-to-day business.
- While this is an issue for consumers, it is also an issue of great importance for banks:
  - Banks face GBP 235 billion in penalties annually.
  - 57% of complaints are resolved in favor of the consumer.
  - Banks are increasing their compliance workforce to meet the demands of increased complaints.
- There are three distinct pain points: (1) a need to identify high-risk areas in lending contracts; (2) lack of training materials for consumers agreeing to lending contracts; and (3) absence of a channel where banks can deliver and audit training materials on lending contracts to consumers.

Week 5: Goals, Content, and Milestone Meeting 1 Overview (Steps 1–2 with a Dash of Step 3)

The goals for this week are for the participants to receive feedback from the Lead Facilitator on progress to date on Steps 1 and 2 (with a dash of Step 3). Additionally, the goal is for participants to learn how to get on the same *Problem Plane* and to prepare a short presentation of the problem that brings it to life in a way that a person external to the team can understand. The hardest part will be the former, because as described in *Leader Upheaval*, teams often believe that they have consensus about what the problem is and who they solving it for but after they write this out individually and then share their statements, they realize that like different airplanes, they may all be heading in the same direction but they are not on the same airplane. This type of vertical separation is death knell to progress and another time I recommend the PM or Lead Facilitator be a Big Bird and point it out and push for convergence. So it is imperative to push this point before moving to the *5 Whys and Root Cause Analysis Exercise* and *Problem Trip Mapping*, that is, chunking and mapping problems into smaller pieces/phases and identifying different stakeholders along the way.

The Lead Facilitator should begin by providing a roadmap for the meeting: The first agenda item is to review the team's progress on the first three steps. The team will have 10 minutes to present and then the Lead Facilitator will ask questions and provide feedback. The team should be reminded that during the presentation, when talking about Step 1, they should be sure to focus on the key stats and research that demonstrates the "need" or "opportunity" and how it impacts who. After the presentation and feedback from the Lead Facilitator, the Lead Facilitator should probe to ensure that individuals are truly on the same *Problem Plane*, which can be done easily virtually by asking each person to type out the problem in their own words into the chat. You will be amazed at the small (and big differences) that are causing confusion (and perhaps strife!). The next agenda item is an exercise designed to better empathize with the target audience: *The 5 Whys and Root Cause Analysis Exercise*. The Lead Facilitator should have a team member record the "Whys" and "AHA" moments in a Google Doc in the team folder.

After conducting that exercise, there should be a discussion about who needs to be contacted to better understand the target audience and other key stakeholders to further refine the problem. They should have already reached out to some people. But now is the time to conduct real 5 Whys Interviews. Explain that before they interview someone, they might want to draft an interview template and review the *Interviewing Tips and Sample Interview Template Resource*. Finally, the meeting should turn to how to map problems with a *Problem Trip Mapping Exercise (Step 2 Focus)*. And, last but not least, the meeting should conclude with a review of the deliverables and goals for the coming week which includes attending or watching a webinar about creating and relaying consumer/user stories.

This week teams should reach out to their Shadow Team to schedule an hour together wherein one team presents their progress to date for 10–15 minutes and the other team provides feedback, and then they swap. These meetings should occur during weeks 9 and 11 but should be calendared now. Also, because there are many people's schedules involved, teams should consider using a calendar tool like Doodle. Although some teams might prefer to only meet with their Shadow Team once vs twice, remember that these meetings are most helpful if they occur prior to the scheduled Milestone Meeting occurring during those weeks. In fact, they are purposefully scheduled during the same weeks as Milestone Meetings so the team can receive feedback from externals and revise accordingly before presenting to the Lead Facilitator.

The following "Retracing Footsteps" shows a Team's *5 Whys and Root Cause Analysis Exercise,* **which, as you will see, sometimes leads to more than five questions that begin with "why".**

RETRACING FOOTSTEPS: SAMPLE 5 WHYS EXERCISE

Step 3: Understanding Key Stakeholders and Target Audience(s)

Example Topic Challenge: Cogito Ergo Sum: *How can cognitive technologies transform the way financial institutions deal with the impact of regulatory change on their consumer lending documentation?*

Narrowed Problem: *There is a rising number of consumer complaints against the bank after the lending process resulting in fines paid by the bank despite the bank actually complied with regulations during the consumer lending process.*

1. Why would the bank pay consumers for noncompliance if they complied?
   - Proving compliance is complicated and difficult, requiring the bank to undergo a hefty procedure in a nonsystematic way.
2. Why is it so difficult?
   - The Ombudsman shifts the burden of proof of compliance to the bank. The deadline to prove compliance tolls once any part of the bank has been notified of the complaint. This often results in banks, although compliant, paying penalties to consumers over an inability to meet the burden on time.
3. Why do the consumers ask for the penalties if the bank complied?
   - Consumers think they were wronged.
4. Why do consumers think they were wronged?
   - They don't really realize what they agreed to when they agreed to it despite the fact that the bank told them repeatedly and it was in writing and they signed, etc.
5. Why don't they realize it if the bank tells them and they sign a document acknowledging that they understand?
   - They don't understand the language that is used by the bank professionals and that is in the lending contracts.

RETRACING FOOTSTEPS: SAMPLE
5 WHYS EXERCISE *(continued)*

---

6. Why don't they understand the language?
   - The topic and language are complex to consumers and the banks do not provide training on lending contracts to ensure consumer understanding and regulation compliance.
7. Why doesn't the process include training?
   - The way the process is structured doesn't really lend itself to delivering training that would be effective.

C. STEP 3: UNDERSTANDING KEY STAKEHOLDERS AND TARGET AUDIENCE(S)

This step is all about finding a very narrow target audience and understanding everything about that target audience. However, to do so, often we have to understand other audiences who have influence or are impacted as well. There are often at least two sides to every story and then other stakeholders that might be impacted or have impact. So multiple key stakeholders may need to be investigated. As discussed further in *Leader Upheaval*, I always tell my participants about my time working at Leo Burnett as an account executive on Kellogg's® Apple Jacks®.[5] It taught me how important it is to see both sides. With Kellogg's® Apple Jacks®, we learned the hard way that marketers have to talk to buyers (moms of tweens) who want to buy healthy cereal AND also the eaters (tweens) who want anything but a healthy cereal. This further investigation into other stakeholders is also important for the team to be able to better empathize and understand the key target audience for whom they are solving the problem. If they don't understand what they are facing in terms of pressures and influences, then they cannot solve their problem for them.

Also, just as we want participants to fall in love with their problems, in this step, we want participants to fall in love with their target audiences. The target audience is the focal point. This is why Amazon's founder Jeff Bezos places one empty chair in each meeting. He does this to represent the customer/user. When we are falling in love, we are obsessed with the person. We want to know everything about them from the small to the big. So understanding who will fill the empty chair requires talking to people in the target audience group and eliciting real-life examples from them (e.g., times and dates and descriptions of the who, what, where, when, and how it happened).

---

[5] Michele DeStefano, Leader Upheaval: A Guide to Client-Centricity, Culture Creation, and Collaboration (ABA Publishing, forthcoming 2023).

Like the falling-in-love stage in our personal lives, in an innovation cycle, this is the time when we explore not only everything about the problem but also everything about the target audience(s): the user(s) experiencing the problem or opportunity and those impacting or influencing the problem. It is at this stage that we create consumer profiles and stories from the point of view of the people who are experiencing the problem or have a need.

So, Step 3 is all about investigating and empathizing with the person who sits in the empty chair. All of this investigation is intended to help the teams understand their target audience to a depth that is beyond what they think they need to know so that the solution that they create is tight and relevant in every way: content, design, process, length, mood, brand, feel, and message. In this step, teams should define the target audience from both sides (sometimes multiple sides) of the problem. Further, eventually the team will need to develop a creative way to bring the consumer stories to life so that the audience is moved, that is, so that the audience feels as passionately as the team does about solving THIS problem for THIS core key audience(s). However, before doing that, the team likely will need to refine the problem again with the *Problem Trip Mapping Exercise (Step 3 Focus)* that includes how and when the different audiences are impacted and a *Consumer/Stakeholder Profile and Problem Refinement Exercise.*

Finally, during Step 3, the team needs to ensure that their target audiences are large enough to justify creating a solution and small enough to test via a pilot or prototype. This is why Step 3 necessarily includes a dash of Step 5. And this goes back to what I call the *Field of Dreams* problem explained in *Leader Upheaval.* Just because you build it, doesn't mean your target audience will come. Also, if your target audience is not large enough, the bleachers will be almost empty and you might not be able to cover the costs of running and maintaining the field. For Step 3, the overarching goals are to:

- Identify one or two discrete target audiences experiencing the problem that are large enough to justify the solution and small enough to test via a pilot/prototype.
- Identify other stakeholders who have influence or who are impacted by the problem.
- Create a client/consumer/user profile and story for each core target audience.

Some of the tools and exercises to help with Step 3 include:

- Secondary research to determine who are the groups of people most impacted by this problem.
  - Ask: Which group is most targetable, reachable?
  - Consider: How large is each universe? How can they be reached?
- Review *Interviewing Tips and Sample Interview Template Resource* to guide investigative research of people in your target audience.
- Primary research, including investigative interviews and/or focus groups of people in your target audience.
- *The 5 Whys and Root Cause Analysis Exercise* to separate root causes from symptoms, refine problems, and better understand and empathize with the target audience(s).

- *Key Stakeholder Analysis Exercise* to identify and prioritize all potential stakeholders (internal and external to the company or firm) that may have a stake in the problem, that may care whether you are pursuing the problem, that may be impacted by the problem or the solution, or that may have influence over the problem or solution.
- *Consumer/Stakeholder Profile and Problem Refinement Exercise* to enhance understanding of each target audience(s)' biography, age, occupation, way of living, expertise, level of education, etc., and further refine the problem
- *Consumer Story Mad Libs® Exercise* to create consumer/user stories for your key target audiences that bring the problem to life from the target audience(s)' point of view.
- *Getting on the Same Problem Plane Exercise* (AGAIN) because after we fine-tune the consumer audience, we need to tweak our problem statement: Is the team really on the same page as to what is the problem and who is experiencing it?
- *Problem Trip Mapping Exercise* (Step 3 Focus) to map the process in which the problem surfaces (which could be along a trajectory or timeline, or it could be an order of how something is accomplished or created), chunk the problem down into smaller parts and map the key audiences impacting/experiencing/creating the narrower problems within the problem and the pain points of the various key audiences (what they are and when they occur), and uncover all the various problems within the problem. (Note: this exercise is also used in Step 2.)
- *Bringing the Consumer Story to Life Resource* to view examples of top-notch consumer stories and create inspiration.
- *CTQ (Critical-to-Quality) Tree Exercise*[6], a diagram-based tool that helps translate broad consumer needs into specific, actionable, measurable performance requirements.

Week 6: Goals, Content, and PM Team Meeting Overview (Step 3)

The goals for week 6 are to gain a better understanding of the problem, sort out the root causes from the symptoms, and gain insight into the pain points of the target audience. Additionally, teams will begin to map their problem into smaller parts along a trajectory and gain a better understanding of the importance and role of the consumer target audience. To that end they will begin to explore different tools and techniques to structure and develop the client/consumer/user story. Additionally, teams will take the time to reflect on their teaming successes to date and participate in a feedback exercise.

Like the last two weeks, the number one job of the PM is STILL to STOP participants from solutionizing. To that end, this week and next week are focused on understanding and empathizing with the target audience experiencing the problem. This is key for the

---

[6] Mind Tools Content Team, *Critical to Quality (CTQ) Trees: Translating Broad Customer Needs into Specific Requirements*, Mindtools, https://www.mindtools.com/pages/article/ctq-trees.htm, (last visited July 9, 2022).

team to refine the problem statement and, also, to create compelling consumer/user stories depicting the problem and how it impacts the consumer/target audience(s). A solution is not yet appropriate.

The roadmap for this meeting should be to have the team share their Investigative Interviews and their progress on *Problem Trip Mapping*. As they share, the PM should try to point out variances and discrepancies in the stories and the problem so that the team knows where to focus and do further investigation. Then the PM should discuss consumer stories and review the *Consumer/Stakeholder Profile and Problem Refinement Exercise* and *Consumer Story Mad Libs® Exercise*. The meeting should conclude with a short feedback session about how the teaming is going so far. I like two different tools for feedback. One is called the *W3 TALA Feedback Exercise* that I learned from Jeff Carr, former general counsel of Univar and also a race car driver. Essentially each person shares the following:

- **W**hat **W**orked **W**ell—that's the W3.
- What they think the teaming should **T**ake **A** **L**ook **A**t—(that's the TALA), which is something that they should improve on when it comes to teaming.

The other feedback tool I like is called the *I Like, I Wish, I Wonder Exercise*—which I learned from Bjarne Tellmann, the general counsel of Haleon (formerly part of GlaxoSmithKline). Each person shares what they *like* about the team/teaming (the positive), what they *wish* was a little bit different about the team/teaming) (the negative), and what they *wonder* that they might do to help the team/teaming (the onus: what part did they contribute to things not working as well as they could have and what can they do to improve the teaming on a go-forward).

At this point, it is a good time to remind the team about the PM role. Likely, the PM has had to repeatedly stop participants from jumping to solutions. Therefore, the PM should remind the team of the Albert Einstein 55-5 approach. If he had an hour to solve your problem, he would spend 55 minutes thinking about the problem and 5 minutes on the solution. This is a tough role to play, and participants often bristle when "interrupted" or "stopped" from explaining solutions or ideas. However, they need this tough love, and it will help them in the future in so many ways (if they truly learn to spend more time on the problem finding before ideating solutions). The PM might bring this up and explain that the PM's role is something like what follows:

> *My job is to make sure that the team is progressing along the 5 Steps in the right way and at the right pace. I was selected for this job because I have experience [describe experience]. Although I hope we build a relationship and that you like me, my role is not to be your friend. Think of me more like a supervisor/manager than a mentor with suggestions. The deliverables were not of my making. They come from this handbook. Right now, my main deliverable is to help you find a narrow problem/target audience that you feel passionately about and that is solvable AND to*

prevent you from ideating/jumping to the solution stage. This requires tough love on my part. If that tough love causes the team to jell and defend against me as a team and, as a result of this, the team is now on the same page as it relates to the problem and/or target audience, then I'm for it!! Also, my job is to take every moment as a teaching moment. This journey is as much about learning how to innovate as it is about transforming how we collaborate and learning new mindsets, skillsets, and behaviors. Therefore, if there is a moment where a participant is not acting collaborative or professional, my role is to give feedback. Of course, individual feedback occurs individually. Also, remember that if you are having trouble teaming or have concerns, please reach out to me or the Lead Facilitator (or the Teaming Coach if you have one). You don't have to specify who or what but simply say you think the team could use a teaming session which can do wonders for team dynamics.

[Then the PM should conclude with something positive about how much they are liking the role and this team.]

And, as always, the PM should end the meeting by sharing the deliverables for the week. They should discuss who will be doing what in the coming week, as there is a lot to do and some of it can be divvied. For example, who will pull together the key data/stats and research supporting the existence and importance of the problem? Hopefully the team has a folder full of this research, but someone needs to pull it together in a cohesive format because each team needs data and stats to support the breadth, heft, and importance of the narrow problem they identified. Who will take the lead in scheduling the team meeting to co-create the *Problem Trip Map*? Who will be in charge of developing and creating the 15-minute presentation for Milestone Meeting 2 and making sure all pieces are in the deck and that parts of the script are divided? Who will reach out to schedule time with the Coach for weeks 10 and 13? Don't forget to remind team members that ideally, the Coach would simply meet with the team during their regular PM Team Meetings but that depends on the Coach's schedule. (Note: the week the team meets with the Coach, there is not an additional PM Meeting and the PM may—but does not have to—attend the meeting between the team and the Coach).

Week 7: Goals, Content, and Milestone Meeting 2 Overview (Steps 2–3 with a Dash of Step 1)

The goals for the week are essentially for teams to put Steps 2 and 3 together. To that end, they should be able to agree on and explain the narrowed problem within the challenge that they are focusing on and illustrate the trajectory of the problem and the various parts of the problem and who is impacted (or influencing the problem) at each stage. Additionally, they should have developed moving consumer stories that illustrate the target audiences that are experiencing or impacted by the narrow problem and that bring the problem to life. Last, they should have nailed Step 1 by now with data, research, and stats that prove their problem exists, that it matters, and that solving it will have a certain type and level of positive impact (or that not solving it will have a certain type and level of negative impact).

During Milestone Meeting 2, participants should have 15 minutes to present their problem (in a few sentences), stats/data/research proving the problem exists and matters, a map illustrating the trajectory of the problem and its parts, and consumer/user stories that bring the problem to life—not necessarily in that order! In fact, I often find that starting with the consumer/user stories is not only the most impactful way to start but also makes the presentation of the problem much clearer from the start. This is because often in the team's problem statements and maps, they have missed some of the parts and pieces that the consumer stories have uncovered. Either way, the point of Milestone Meeting 2 is to identify any missing parts (or extraneous parts that don't fit the narrow problem). So the Lead Facilitator's feedback should focus on those items as well as asking a lot of questions about the problem and the consumer stories.

Inevitably, most teams will need to revise their consumer/user stories and likely have to do a few more investigative interviews as needed. Additionally, in this meeting, doing the *Getting on the Same Problem Plane Exercise* again is essential at the end of the meeting. This is because after all the feedback and poking holes, various participants might have changed their minds slightly on where the team is or *should be* focusing. Again, importantly, there should be no solutionizing in this meeting. Beware of the problem statements and consumer/user stories that deliver or hint at a solution. Although it is true that in the *Consumer Story Mad Libs® Exercise*, there is a portion that requires describing what the consumer *would like* instead of the problem they are experiencing, this should only hint toward *a* solution—lead a horse to water—but not actually describe *the* solution—at least not yet!

As always, the meeting should close with an overview of the deliverables for the coming week, emphasizing that the team needs to get on the same *Problem Plane*, refine their consumer stories, and meet as a team to ideate because in the next week's PM Meeting, they need to informally present all of this—including one or more possible solutions. This should actually be like music to their ears because finally they are allowed to do what the PM has prevented them from doing so far: problem solving!

Last, the teams need to be reminded that if they are going to schedule the optional expert meeting with a Business Planning or Pitching expert for week 10 and/or a Branding or Tech Engineering Expert for week 12, they should reach out this week to schedule it so it is calendared. (Note: they can invite the expert(s) to attend the scheduled PM Meeting week 12 if that is easier).

The next "Retracing Footsteps" provides the results from a team conducting the *Consumer/Stakeholder Profile and Problem Refinement Exercise* **and** *Consumer Story Mad Libs® Exercise.*[7]

---

[7] These consumer stories were greatly aided by Erika Pagano, former Director of LawWithoutWalls and currently the Head of Legal Innovation and Design at Simmons & Simmons Wavelength.

RETRACING FOOTSTEPS: SAMPLE CONSUMER PROFILES AND STORIES

Step 3: Understanding Key Stakeholders and Target Audience(s)

Example Topic Challenge: Cogito Ergo Sum: *How can cognitive technologies transform the way financial institutions deal with the impact of regulatory change on their consumer lending documentation?*

Results from Consumer/Stakeholder Profile and Problem Refinement Exercise:

- Understanding the audience:
  - Banks were:
    - Facing a growing number of consumer complaints as lending products and accompanying documentation grew in sophistication.
    - Struggling to prove compliance on time.
    - Paying penalties unnecessarily (banks complied with regulations but were unable to prove it in part because they did not have a standardized, easy process to pull together compliance evidence).
  - Consumers were:
    - Signing contracts without understanding the terms.
    - Feeling confused, frustrated, angry.
    - Filing complaints against the bank with the Ombudsman.

Consumer/user stories from the *Consumer Story Mad Libs® Exercise*:

- Banks: Francis Finance is an officer at a big bank in London. He is well-educated, accomplished, and well-paid in his serious career. He wakes up each morning at 5:30, dons an impeccably pressed suit and tie, and dashes out the door by 7 for a quick 30-minute tube ride to the office. Without fail, he purchases a flat white on the ground floor of his office tower—a final moment of Zen before the whizzes, whirs, dings, and chirps of the business day begin. He's already answered a few critical emails during his commute and is ready to make headway through his inbox at his desk when—*ding!*, followed by a long sigh—a frequent and flustering pet peeve appears yet again. The Ombudsman is levying a fine on the bank, alleging it did not comply with the terms of a loan agreement following a complaint by a consumer who said they were confused. "But we did comply! The consumer didn't listen!" thinks an exasperated Francis. "We did everything we were supposed to. We literally followed the law to a T. The tough part is proving it. I simply can't get into the head of each consumer and force them to understand and somehow record it all. If only there was a solution, so much time and effort spent going through this same circus over and over and over—not to mention wasting money on needless fines AND the

(continued)

RETRACING FOOTSTEPS: SAMPLE CONSUMER PROFILES AND STORIES *(continued)*

frustration, stress, and decrease in productivity this brings me—could all be fixed." Francis shakes his head in disbelief, feeling heavy with the knowledge that the promise of a new day has just been derailed by an unnecessary, unfortunately routine, entirely preventable problem. What he would like is a different process, perhaps even automated, that would help him ensure that the consumer really understood what they were signing and that prevented them from being able to win baseless claims that they did not.

- **Consumers:** Charlie Consumer lives in the English countryside. He's a father of three with a small yet steadily busy handyman business. He took out a loan from a big bank in the hopes of growing his service into a small home improvement business. With one more baby along the way, Charlie wants to do all he can to provide for his family. Although Charlie is smart, finance isn't his jam. He knew he had to sign some papers in the loan process, but he's still not exactly sure—even though he already has the money—how this whole thing works. What must he do as the loan recipient? What are his rights? What duties does the bank owe him? What must he do in order to not default? What does the bank have a right to take in case he defaults? This string of questions often keeps Charlie up at night. Charlie wishes it wasn't so confusing, and he hopes he's taking all the right steps and making the correct payments. After all, the future of his family's well-being is on the line. He is confused and frustrated because he feels like he owes more money than he had planned. He tries calling the bank. No one answers. Eventually, he just files a complaint because that's the only recourse he can find on the website. He didn't have adequate time or an explanation in a language that he understood nor an understanding of the longer-term financial implications of how the loan works. What he would like is to not have felt rushed and pressured when signing the loan and he would have liked to be able to ask questions without feeling stupid. What he wishes is that he had really understood what he was getting into BEFORE he signed.

D. STEP 4: SOLVING THE PROBLEM AND PROTOTYPING

The good news is that Step 4 is all about ideating and this is the step that it seems the team has been dying to reach from the beginning. But it hopefully hasn't happened before now because if it has, it likely hasn't resulted in a very positive result! Without a thorough understanding of the problem and its component parts and the multiple stakeholders impacted and influencing the problem and identification of the minimum viable solution (MVS, i.e., the minimum number of component parts that need to be solved), likely the solution the team comes up with won't resonate. Luckily, Step 4 has many different exercises designed to help teams come up with good ideas, many of which emphasize the importance of thinking INSIDE the box, not only outside the box.[8] After all, we all usually work with restraints. Instead of seeing restraints as barriers, we try to use them to set us free in ideation. For example, doing a *Divergent Wild Idea Generation Exercise* and then picking your worst idea and trying to improve it, or making a list of all your favorite apps on your phone and then picking one and trying to use its attributes to solve your problem, can sometimes help us be more creative. This is a type of exaptation discussed in *Leader Upheaval* and *Legal Upheaval*. A great example of this is doctors who created a jelly-like pill to monitor tumors by adopting the attributes of the puffer fish. Like other design thinkers, I wholeheartedly support using successes in other fields, industries, or even other areas of our own companies to help solve the team's problem. And so, Step 4 includes some of my own exercises along with some of those other design thinkers' exercises that do just that, that is, combine or imitate successes for our own ideation benefit.

Step 4 also includes exercises designed to help refine the teams' initial ideas, because research shows that our first ideas are usually not our best ones. And sometimes, the solutions we come up with already exist or the opposite, they aren't viable or feasible or they only take into account one side of the story. In this way, Step 4 requires a look back to Steps 2 and 3 and a look forward to Step 5 regarding viability and business planning. People often think finding the solution (Step 4) is the hardest part, but it should be the easiest. If the team has done Steps 2 and 3 right (and multiple times, including *Problem Trip Mapping*, a *Consumer/Stakeholder Profile and Problem Refinement Exercise*, and an *MVS Steeple People Exercise*), the solution follows almost naturally. The time spent on refining the problem and the consumer stories enables the brains to percolate. Then when the team is truly ready to solutionize, the solution *pops pops pops* like the AHA moments we have in the shower. But although it might feel that way, the reality is that the ideas have been simmering. One person's thoughts have spurred another person's thoughts. This migration is what Stephen Johnson calls the slow hunch theory that leads to the "pearl of the oyster."[9] As he points out: "There are good ideas, and then there are good ideas that make it easier to have other good ideas."[10] This is another reason why exaptation is a critical concept of Step 4. This is also why we need to beware the team's inclination to go with their first idea (which, as said, is rarely the best) and instead make sure the team members build on each other's ideas to reach that pearl.

I find the hardest part for teams is narrowing the solution so that it truly is an MVS. Sometimes in the ideation phase, teams forget to solutionize for the narrow problem at hand

---

[8] *See* Drew Boyd & Jacob Goldenberg, Inside the Box: A Proven System of Creativity for Breakthrough Results (2014).

[9] Steven Johnson, Where Good Ideas Come From: The Natural History of Innovation 159–161 (Riverhead Books, 2010).

[10] *Id.* at 243.

and there is scope creep. This is why I love having teams do the *MVS Steeple People Exercise* because it makes sure that if the team identifies three issues that need to be addressed, the solution should address those three and fit like a glove. Anything more might be a bell or whistle (that goes into the steeple) to be saved for after a pilot test of the MVP.

To prevent scope creep and prepare the team for the prototyping that also occurs in Step 4, I have all teams conduct a *Flushing Out the Solution Exercise* to help ensure all components of the solution are mapped out. After that, teams need to create a prototype and a user journey map to show the user experience journey with its solution/prototype.

Also, before spending too much time perfecting the solution and prototype, teams need to move even further into Step 5 to do some business planning, research the competitive landscape, and assess viability.

After they do that, they can return to Step 4 to improve their prototype. And part of improving it is developing a brand. Eventually as well, in Step 4, teams will create a logo, tagline, and a short elevator pitch describing the solution. I like to use my *A-Brand-and-Solution-in-a-Sentence-or-2 Exercise* for that.

Essentially, we spend almost two thirds of the 4-month cycle redefining and solving the problem (Steps 1–3). Then we spend the last one third ideating and prototyping (Step 4) and, of course, testing, business-case planning, and refining the solution (Step 5), which is not only the most time intensive step, but, in some ways, the most important. The overarching goals of Step 4 are to create a solution and prototype and to determine the following:

- What form(s) or manifestation(s) will or can the solution take?
- What will it "do"?
- How many parts/processes should the solution have?
- How does it work, when does it work, and which parts solve which parts of the problem?
- What is the user interface and experience?
- What should the solution's look, feel, and formation be?
- What is your solution's unique selling proposition (i.e., how is your solution different than the competition and how does it add value)?
- What is the solution's brand? What are its physical brand attributes, and its rational and emotional brand benefits? And what is its brand image/personality?

Some of the tools and exercises to help with Step 4 include:

- *Divergent Wild Idea Generation Exercise* to ideate without constraints and without critique to begin generating solution possibilities.
- *Random Objects Association Exercise* to associate and add to ideation by including attributes of random objects.
- *Ideating Inside the Box Exaptation Exercise* to exapt attributes of other phone apps or tech tools that we use and love in order develop or improve a solution.

- *Exploiting Success Exercise* to conduct convergent ideation by multiplying, dividing, subtracting, or adding.[11]
- *Best Idea/Worst Idea Exercise*[12] to explore how to open our minds to solutions to problems even when those solutions appear on their surface as bad or crazy ideas.
- *What I Love Most Exercise* to help refine/further develop the solution and prototype, and start thinking about branding.
- *Attributes Ask Exercise* to ensure that your solution contains the attributes that are expected (given your problem statement) and that are desired (given your consumer stories).
- *Applying the "SCAMPER Technique"*, to ideate by (S) Substituting, (C) Combining, (A) Adapting, (M) Modifying, (P) Putting to another use, (E) Eliminating, and (R) Reversing.[13]
- *Insight Matrix Exercise*[14] to help teams engage in "intelligent recombination," that is, to select and combine past successes with new areas/fields.
- *Scene-by-Scene Flowchart Prototyping Exercise* to begin the prototyping process.
- *Prototyping Examples Resource* to better understand the various forms a prototype can take, for example, storyboard, mock website, wireframe, mockup of how the process/product will work and be used by the user/consumer.
- *User Journey Mapping Examples and Tools Resource* to help teams create a consumer journey map that visualizes exactly how the user will interface with the solution and how the solution will work step by step.
- *MVS Steeple People Exercise* to ensure the team creates a Minimum Viable Solution that fits like a glove with only the minimum number parts and without unnecessary add-ons (i.e., bells and whistles).
- *Flushing Out the Solution Exercise* to determine what are the key features of the solution, the barriers that need to be overcome for implementation, budget and resources, and timing and metrics for success.
- *Problem and Solution Refinement Exercise* to gauge whether the solution the team created solves the problem snugly and whether the problem they have identified and presented is clear to listeners of a pitch.

---

[11] This exercise is based on learnings from DREW BOYD & JACOB GOLDENBERG, *supra* note 7.

[12] This exercise is exapted from TINA SEELIG, WHAT I WISH I KNEW WHEN I WAS 20: A CRASH COURSE ON MAKING YOUR PLACE IN THE WORLD 37–39 (2009).

[13] BOB EBERLE, SCAMPER: CREATIVE GAMES AND ACTIVITIES FOR IMAGINATION DEVELOPMENT (2008); *see also* Fariq Elmansy, *A Guide to the SCAMPER Technique for Creative Thinking*, DESIGNORATE.COM (Apr. 10, 2015), https://www.designorate.com/a-guide-to-the-scamper-technique-for-creative-thinking/.

[14] I exapted this exercise from these two sources: Ken Favaro with Nadim Yacteen, *The Right Ideas in All the Wrong Places*, STRATEGY+BUSINESS (Mar. 11, 2013), https://www.strategy-business.com/article/cs00007 and WILLIAM DUGGAN, CREATIVE STRATEGY: A GUIDE FOR INNOVATION 40–52 (2013).

- *My Favorite Brand Exercise*[15] to instigate teams thinking about branding and client/consumer centricity
- *Brand Matrix Exercise*[16] to help develop a brand for the solution and identify the solution's physical brand attributes, rational and emotional brand benefits, and the brand image/personality.
- *A-Brand-and-Solution-in-a-Sentence-or-2 Exercise* to succinctly describe the branded solution, highlighting its point of difference and benefits and also what it does, for whom, and why.

The following "Retracing Footsteps" is an example of the initial ideation thinking process and a first stab at *A-Brand-and-a-Solution-in-a-Sentence-or-2 Exercise*.

RETRACING FOOTSTEPS: SAMPLE IDEATION

Step 4: Solving the Problem

Example Topic Challenge: Cogito Ergo Sum: *How can cognitive technologies transform the way financial institutions deal with the impact of regulatory change on their consumer lending documentation?*

- **Ideating the Solution:** The team thought about technologies that could easily be reached and used by both main parties (banks and consumers). They settled on an online platform, as it would be easily accessed by the consumer, easily customizable by the bank based on content and branding, and enable lending product training.
- **A-Brand-and-a-Solution-in-a-Sentence-or-2:** Clear Loan is an online training tool to help banks reduce consumer-borrower complaints and educate consumer-borrowers on the terms and conditions of their lending documentation. With increased consumer understanding of lending documentation the number of complaints lodged will decrease thereby reducing the burden on banks to prove compliance.

Week 8: Goals, Content, and PM Team Meeting Overview (Step 4 with a Dash of Step 5)

The main goal for the week is for the teams to come up with some solutions to their problem. To do that, however, they must do some more work on Steps 2 and 3. Specifically, before ideating, teams need to (1) refine consumer/user stories that illustrate the target audience(s) that are experiencing the narrow problem (Step 3), and (2) create consensus on the exact wording of the team's narrowed problem, target audience(s), and reasons "why" this problem needs solving, that is, via a *Getting on the Same Problem Plane Exercise* (Step 2). After that, they then should partake in the *Insight Matrix Exercise* during their own team meeting (without the PM) to identify some possible solutions to their narrow

---

[15] This exercise was co-developed with Anita Ritchie, the Director of LawWithoutWalls.

[16] This exercise was developed by Anita Ritchie, Director of LawWithoutWalls.

challenge. This should all be done prior to the PM Meeting so that during the PM Team Meeting, the team can relay informally, in 10–15 minutes, its progress through Steps 1–4, including their *Problem Plane* statement, a set of consumer/user stories that illustrates the narrow problem the team seeks to address for their target audience, and at least one (but possibly more) solutions to the problem.

The good news is that this PM Meeting should be fun because it is all about reviewing the team's progress in the first four steps. And finally, we can talk about solutions! However, in doing so, please keep Step 5 in mind because some ideas may not survive the monitoring and reflection that occurs in Step 5. Also, the team may be experiencing "group-think" and not see the holes that the PM might. Challengingly, sometimes they come up with solutions that already exist, which is again why a little bit of Step 5 from the PM is essential. Moreover, often teams become wed to their first idea, but please remind them again: the first idea is rarely the best idea. Experts contend that teams should brainstorm over 100 ideas to get to the ideas that are novel.[17] Also, be prepared for solutions that don't fit the problem, that is, they solve for more than the narrow problem statement or they solve for something totally different than the problem they posed. Also beware: We shouldn't hear "new" problems in the solution that weren't already identified.

If new or different problems are introduced in the solution (as opposed to PRIOR to introducing the solution) the PM should point this out during the PM's feedback session. The PM should feel free to do the *Getting on the Same Problem Plane Exercise* again if needed or better yet, an *MVS Steeple People Exercise*.

Also, at this point, the ideas will not be completely flushed out so the teams need to be pushed to think about how this idea would really work, who would use it, when, and why? The PM can refer to their Problem Trip Map. Where on the Problem Trip Map are they solving and for whom? If this is fuzzy, then the team might need to work on that map more in the following week, which might require more investigative interviews. Also, they need to be thinking about Step 5 some, that is, they need to begin to consider who would pay for this service or product, what kind of funding model would work, and when would it be profitable? Does tech exist that could make it happen? Sometimes teams come up with a solution that isn't viable or practical or valuable or that is before its time from a tech standpoint. Sometimes teams are stuck on their first idea (which, I repeat on purpose, is often not the best idea!). Thus, for the coming week, we assign a splash of Step 5, a *Pre-Mortem Exercise* wherein the teams ask: What could go wrong? Imagine the worst-case scenario. Who and what stands in the way? What are the risks and weaknesses?

Of course, we don't want to quell their enthusiasm too much and if the team is hanging on to their first idea or the PM wants to move the team from their current idea which the PM thinks is "bad" to a better idea, I recommend using an ideation exercise I call *Best Idea/Worst Idea* which I have borrowed and exapted from Stanford Professor

---

[17] *See, e.g.*, Tina Seelig, *Innovation Demands Focus and Reframing*, https://www.youtube.com/watch?v=HHbS1YDhsBg.

Tina Seelig and is described in one of her books.[18] This exercise is designed to open attendees' minds to the concept that there are no bad ideas in collaborative brainstorming and that sometimes, when we are constrained and forced to think "inside the box," we can be even more creative than without any boundaries or restraints. Professional service providers are often giving other people's problems—and other people's solutions. This exercise teaches them not only that what we think is our best idea may not always be our best idea but also how to make lemons out of lemonade, that is, how to take a different team's worst idea and turn it into something really great. It also teaches them that with the right frame of mind (creative, inclusive, adaptive, and "Yes And . . ."), we can collaborate to find the seeds of possibility in the craziest, silliest ideas. This powerful mindset transforms the biggest challenges into the biggest opportunities.

Each PM will have their own style for how they provide feedback to the team. That said, because the PMs have likely interrupted the teams in the past (many times) to stop them from ideating, now that the teams are finally allowed to present their ideas, my suggestion is to let the participants complete their entire informal presentation before providing any feedback. Also, I recommend using the *I Like, I Wish, I Wonder Exercise* for feedback on their presentations (mentioned above during week 6). I like this tool because it starts with a positive and it helps provide vision without seeming overly directive. At some point, the PM might have to be directive, but hopefully today, the PM will not have to be. Last, some teams won't have a solution today and those that do, will likely need to improve them. Therefore, there is an ideation exercise for this meeting that can help.

After the team presents and the PM provides feedback on all parts but especially to help them assess the strengths and weaknesses of their solutions, the PM might start by asking them to explain the results of their *Insight Matrix Exercise*. This may help the PM decide which ideation exercise will help the team the most in the remaining time together to refine their solution or start over and solutionize from scratch. There are multiple options of ideation exercises available, as listed above and in the Appendix of Exercises, the instructions for which can be found on either of my websites: micheledestefano.com or movelaw.com. Some good ones to start off with are *Ideating Inside the Box Exaptation Exercise* or *Divergent Wild Idea Generation Exercise* or *Exploiting Success Exercise*. If the team seems on the right path, the PM might consider the *Random Objects Association Exercise* to help push their solutionizing. Whichever exercise is selected, the PM might preface it with some background as follows: *One of the hardest things about going on an innovation journey is coming up with a really great idea that is viable, marketable, and fundable! In many design thinking books, how to come up with that great idea is never explained. This exercise is designed to help you come up with that great idea or if your idea already has legs, to improve it.*

---

[18] TINA SEELIG, *supra* note 12.

As always, the PM should provide an overview of the deliverables for the coming week which includes attending or watching a webinar about prototyping and to continue ideating and flushing their solutions as a team (using the various exercises the PM recommends from the list) with the goal of coming up with two to three ideas that seem viable. The PM should remind them of the purpose of their upcoming Shadow Team Meeting: to practice pitching, and giving and receiving feedback. During that meeting, as mentioned, one team presents their progress to date for 10-15 minutes and the other team provides feedback, and then they swap. And remind them that their Shadow Team Meeting is in ADDITION to the upcoming Milestone Meeting 3 next week for which they need to prepare a 10-15 minute presentation that covers Steps 1–4 (but not necessarily in that order!). Instead, the team should think about how best to bring the problem to life. Perhaps start with a consumer story (Step 3), then share a detailed problem statement (Step 4). Then move to the stats/research showing why this problem matters and what a difference a solution can make (Step 1). These three parts should ensure that the two to three ideas (Step 4) they present to solve the problem spread like butter i.e., flow naturally from the detailed presentation of the problem and main issues that need to be solved.

Week 9: Goals, Content, and Milestone Meeting 3 Overview (Steps 1–4 with a Dash of Step 5)

The goals for the week are essentially for teams to focus on refining their solutions and begin developing prototypes with a focus on Step 4 and a dash of Step 5. The reason teams meet with their Shadow Team and, later, with the Lead Facilitator is that in these meetings they will be pushed from their group-think and from a very common mistake wherein teams come up with a solution, but do not really think through how it will really work, who will use it, when, and why. Often, at the beginning, the solutions teams pitch are too vague (or at least they are described in so vague a way that you cannot really understand what the solution does). As well, once the team starts solutionizing, they sometimes start to put things in the solution that they never mentioned in the problem. In other words, sometimes their problem statements become weaker than they were before. The good news is they can be made stronger because in solutionizing they have discovered more parts of the problem that needed solving, but then the problem statements and consumer stories need to be revised to match. Let me give you an example.

Recently, at the LawWithoutWalls Sprint, one of the teams was super-disappointed that they didn't win any of the awards. They were sure that they had a fantastic problem and solution. And they did. Indeed, after Sprint, they have received approval from the most senior people at the sponsoring pharmaceutical company to bring the solution to fruition which was a new process to contract with facilities for clinical trials so that lifesaving-drugs could go to market faster. However, the problem was, the team didn't do a great job at explaining what the problem was before introducing the solution. Instead, they used complex and/or vague descriptions and hid parts of the problem within the solution description. The flow of the presentation was as follows: After explaining what a clinical trial was and how important it was to the drug manufacturing process, the team described what is a clinical trial *agreement*, i.e., contract: "The clinical trial agreement is the contract between the pharmaceutical company, and the study-site which defines the various conditions of the clinical trial. This is in order to protect the pharma company, the institution participating, and of course, the patients. The clinical trial agreement is therefore a critical part of this process." They then moved into describing the problem: "Although clearly needed, the clinical trial agreement is often perceived as more of an administrative burden than something which actually drives any value. To this end, it has received large amounts of pressure from within pharmaceutical divisions to cut time to execution and stop holding up drugs going to market." Notice that they say how the contract is perceived but they speak so generally and do not include real people in the story. We do not know who is perceiving the contracting process as a burden or who is being pressured. And we do not know why it is taking too much time to execute and how the current process is holding things up or by whom. If the audience does not understand exactly how the contract is created, negotiated, and approved and what parties are involved, they aren't ready for a solution. Unfortunately, it isn't until the team presented the solution that the audience learned that the problem is, in part, due to poorly informed first drafts of contracts and the people experiencing the problem are the contract managers (who are not lawyers) and that they aren't able to fix the problem on their own due to lack of workflow tracking and knowledge sharing. The problem with learning this in the solution description is that it is confusing to the audience which is the opposite of what is desired. The solution part of a pitch should spread like butter. By the time you present it, your audience should be ready, chomping at the bit, really. They should feel as passionate as you about solving this problem and they should have a real understanding of the problem's nooks and crannies so the solution fits like a glove, which is what the *MVS Steeple People Exercise* is designed to do. It asks you to imagine that each of the parts of the problem that the team is solving is a finger, the solution should cover each finger like a glove does. And yes it limits teams to five parts. Again we want an MVS and we want to think tiny as explained in *Leader Upheaval* for that is the best way to pilot an innovation.

As recommended to the PM last week, if scope-creep happens during the Milestone Meeting this week, and there is time, then initiate an *MVS Steeple People Exercise*. Or, instead, they could do a *Flushing Out the Solution Exercise*, which requires consideration of Steps 4 and 5 in tandem. It asks: What is the solution? What does it do? What are the key assets/ features that must be included to be successful? How does it work and who does it work for and who else will be involved? Why does this solution need to be implemented now and why should you or your firm do so? What barriers will need to be overcome for buy-in and implementation? What budget and resources (external or internal) will be needed (i.e., how much time and money and whose time and money)? And note: they likely won't finish this during this Milestone Meeting, but they should continue to work on it as it is assigned for the week to come. So it is not wasted time to get started!

The Lead Facilitator might also ask them to tell you what the team learned from their Shadow Team Meeting.

Last, if the solution is still not really "there-there," this is a good time to go back to the *Problem Trip Mapping Exercise* or conduct an exercise that helps them add on to and enhance their solution. I like to conduct what I have named the *What I Love Most Exercise* because it does all of this and it also gets the team thinking about branding and client/consumer-centricity. Essentially, I have them each jot down what they love most about their favorite service experience, their favorite product, their best learning experience, and their favorite brand. Then I ask them to pick a few of the answers to exapt into their solution: How might they exapt some of the attributes/qualities that they love the most in these unrelated categories to make their solution better? Here is an example: I played this game with my son, Trip. The service experience he loved the most was at Subway (a sandwich food chain) and his reasons were (1) it is quick; (2) the workers always remembered his name with a smile; and (3) he could order his sub sandwich any way he wanted. How might the students' current solution be improved by making it faster? How might it be improved by making it personalized or more personal? How might they customize the solution and give the target audience more choices? How might they "remember" their audience and make them feel good when they use the solution they created? Oh now, I'm thinking about collecting data, and metrics, oh and maybe even selling the data . . . Ahhh! so this exercise can also help with Step 5! The Lead Facilitator should be sure to point that out because, after all, they were supposed to read Step 5 and keep it in mind all week while solutionizing.

Two final words of caution about the team's solution: First, be sure to ask if they did their competition research. Has someone else already created this solution? Second, remember the *Field of Dreams* problem mentioned earlier. Even though the team has only dipped their toes into Step 5, it is important that the size of the market/opportunity is large enough to justify bringing the solution to life. Even if they pass that hurdle, ensure the solution is one that people will be able to "find" and want to "find" and use. Remember just because you build it, it doesn't mean they will come. I always refer to the "graveyard of tech tools" that all companies and firms have to explain this point: Just because it is there, doesn't mean people will use it.

Also, it may be that one of the teams just doesn't have a solution at all that is viable. In that case, they should be reminded of the importance of looking outward. Are there successes in other industries or even at their own firm that they might exapt (which is a bit different than outright imitation)? Remember what was discussed at length in *Leader Upheaval*: exaptation truly is the greatest form of flattery and many famous artists have done it like Mozart, Beethoven, and the Beatles. A great quote by T.S. Eliot sums this up aptly: "Immature poets imitate; mature poets steal; bad poets deface what they take, and good poets make it into something better, or at least something different."[19]

The Lead Facilitator should close the meeting with an overview of the deliverables for the week which entails a focus on Step 5. Teams should attend or watch a webinar about business plans. Further, teams have their first session with their Coach this coming week and an optional meeting with the Business Planning or Pitching Expert. The Lead Facilitator should provide some directions to the teams as to how to handle these meetings. First, they should email a current *Problem Plane* statement, consumer stories, and draft description of the solution and any progress on their business plan to the Coach and/or Expert prior to the meetings. Second, they should spend only the first 10 minutes pitching their Project of Worth (with a slide deck) and then let the rest of the hour focus on questions, feedback and advice from the Coach or Expert. Note: If the team is not going to meet with an expert this week, they should consider pitching their problem and solution to someone external to the firm or company. This is because they need to test and re-assess their solution, problem statement, and understanding of the target audiences which is what Step 5 is all about.

E.   STEP 5: PLANNING, ASSESSING, AND TESTING THE SOLUTION

Step 5 is the last step, but it is the step that has existed in the background throughout and almost never ends. Think iPhone. We are constantly receiving updates that actually are mini-Step 5 tests to improve our user experience but also to test a new update to see if it enhances our experience or increases profitability for Apple. Likewise, this step is not just about testing the substance (the feasibility) of the solution, but also about testing the viability—and the branding and positioning—with the target audience. Assessment is critical to this step. Therefore, there are many opportunities for such assessment. Teams dip their toes into Step 5 (while in Step 4) when they pitch and test the prototype (and branding) they have developed with people internal and external to the organization. Now, they put both feet into Step 5.

Although many people find the amount of meetings in The 3-4-5 Method™ to be daunting at first, the main reason we have so many meetings is that they serve as part of the assessment process that is so important to Step 5. So all the steps (and meetings) are integrated with Step 5. In fact, during Step 5, the teams have to keep refining the problem (Step 2) and their description of their target audience(s) (Step 3) as they learn more and more. In this

---

[19] Good Reads, https://www.goodreads.com/quotes/7832410-immature-poets-imitate-mature-poets-steal-bad-poets-deface-what (last visited May 8, 2023).

way, Step 5 is really occurring throughout the process during the various Milestone Meetings, Coach sessions, Shadow Team Meetings, and the Optional Expert Meetings (with Branding, Tech Engineering, Business Planning, or Pitching experts). These meetings are opportunities to pitch, test, and receive assessment and feedback to go back and refine.

In Step 5, teams create a timeline and action plan to create the solution. They also develop the business case. It's interesting because as happily as professional service providers do the first part is how unhappily they do the second. Yet it is only by creating that business plan that the team can really assess the strengths, weaknesses, opportunities, and threats (SWOT). The two go hand in hand.

The business plan doesn't have to be long and, depending on your needs, a one- or two-page business plan might be sufficient. However, it is important that teams make a business plan that identifies its business model (and return on investment) and projects the date in the future by when the solution will be profitable, what expertise will be needed on the team, potential sources for funding, revenue streams, and the costs for marketing, production, sales, development, operations, etc. Additionally, a thorough understanding and assessment of the competition along with identifying the solution's unique point of difference is essential.

The good news is that, by the time teams fully dive into Step 5, they have already developed many parts of the standard business plan in the prior steps. For example, in Steps 2 and 3 (with a backward dip into Step 1), they have already identified their target market, market needs, and size of market opportunity. And in Step 4, they have identified how they will solve their target audience's problems with a unique value proposition and they have taken a look at the competition (via a dash of this step, Step 5).

The pieces that are left now require a bit more financial analysis. They include (but are not limited to):

- Funding needs/cost structure (running costs/operating expenses, and funding needs/startup investment required)
- Fixed costs (salaries, rents, utilities, costs to develop/create solution)
- Variable costs
- Economies of scale or scope
- Revenue streams, including usage fee, subscription fee, licensing, brokerage fee, advertising, asset/data sale, fixed or dynamic pricing
- Sales and marketing plan (where and how you will promote and convert customers, including distribution paths; will training be required?)
- Key partners (i.e., if selling a product, a partner might be who manufactures the product, who distributes it, and/or who promotes it)
- The team (who needs to be on the team, what qualities/skills/experiences should they have?)

- Metrics, milestones, and timing including key numbers that indicate success, e.g., KPIs (Key Perfomance Indicators) and a roadmap for roll-out that lays out how long the solution will take to be created, piloted, and then rolled out over time and an action plan to get there; also consider by when you will break even and by when you will become profitable

Also included in Step 5 is a focus on developing scripting, storytelling, presentation, and communication skills. Participants have to learn how to put together a beautiful slide deck and a compelling, engaging presentation that brings the consumer story and problem to life in a clear and succinct way to outsiders who know nothing about the topic. Participants have to ensure they set up the problem so that the solution fits like a glove and that they describe the prototype simply and clearly—which is so very hard! Participants also have to learn how to present out loud in front of different types of professionals and different sizes of audiences, sometimes in front of hundreds of people (without notes) with powerful presencing, clear oration, and an absence of "umms," "you-knows," and other ticks.

Rehearsals (and the art of giving and receiving feedback) are key to this step. For many, this last part (the rehearsal and presentation part) is the hardest. Although professional service providers of varying levels of expertise are called on to present in their jobs all the time, an idea pitch like this is a different type of presenting with a different purpose and, therefore, a different style (not to mention that the stakes are often high, the judges and audience are often very senior, and the number of people can be in the hundreds).

One reason we love to use the Ignite Presentation format is because it is so very hard: Self-moving slides, 5 minutes or less; and what makes it even harder is that these presentations are made by the team—collaboratively. Everyone on the team presents so, therefore, there needs to be a lot of coordinating, staging, rehearsing, and trust. Once the slide is gone, you have to stop talking and turn it over to the next person.

The rehearsals and the ConPosium are a big part of Step 5 and require a high level of openness, flexibility, humility, and vulnerability—core skills that we are focusing on honing in the Skills Delta. So, Step 5, in addition to stretching professionals when it comes to financial planning, also stretches them in the middle level of the Skills Delta. The overarching goals of Step 5 are to:

- Assess the strengths, weaknesses, threats, and opportunities of the team's solution.
- Build a business case and plan in its entirety (as noted above), including understanding the competitive landscape and the solution's unique selling proposition, creating a timeline and plan for piloting the solution to a small audience to start, and creating not only a financial plan (with predictions of costs, sales, and ROI) but also a marketing plan.
- Revisit Steps 3 and 4 to refine the problem and solution as needed.
- Test the prototype internally and externally and refine as needed.
- Test the branding and positioning (so as to refine it).
- Create a pitch deck, script, and ConPosium presentation (and enhance communication, storytelling, and presentation skills along the way!).

Some of the tools and exercises to help with Step 5 include:

- *A Pre-Mortem Exercise* to prevent groupthink so that the more likely threats/weaknesses of a project are identified early on.
- *Business Planning SWOT and Competition Analysis Exercise* to identify the key strengths, weaknesses, opportunities, and threats and ensure that the team understands the competition.
- *Creating a One Page Business Plan and Then Some Exercise* to create a business case and plan.
- *Business Planning Checklist Resource* to ensure all components of the business plan are included.
- *Sample Business Plans Resource* to provide examples of business plans.
- *Show Don't Tell, 5 Parts of Effective Storytelling Exercise*[20] to help teams create beautiful decks and present their Projects of Worth in a compelling format.
- *Storytelling and Scripting "Challenger Sale" Exercise*[21] to help teams create moving stories, and a succinct, compelling script.
- *Storytelling, Scripting, and Deck Development Tips Resource* to provide tips to teams for how to create beautiful decks, moving stories, and a succinct compelling script.
- *Powerful Presencing Tips Resource* to provide tips for how to best present and own the stage without upstaging your teammates.
- *Rehearsals Dos and Don'ts, Including Q&A Tips Resource* for tips on how to run rehearsals so that they are effective and help the teams move forward, and to provide tips on how to answer questions and respond to judges' feedback and how NOT to answer questions and respond to judges' feedback.
- *Superhero Presentation Power Tricks Exercise* to share what each team member individually does immediately before a presentation to get revved up and ready so teammates can exapt other teammates tips to source the energy they need to rock this final presentation!
- *Personal Branding Mad Libs® Exercise* to self-reflect on our individual attributes, goals, and aspirations and learn how to create a personal branding statement and to effectively communicate your brand to connect with clients, pitch ideas, and influence stakeholders generally but also at the ConPosium.

An example of a Team's revisions to its solution (Step 4) and refined understanding of the problem and target audiences (Steps 2 and 3) after attending Milestone Meeting 3 and a Shadow Team Meeting and conducting a *Pre-Mortem Exercise* is shown in the next "Retracing Footsteps."

---

[20] This exercise was developed by Anita Ritchie, the Director of LawWithoutWalls.

[21] Exapted from Phyllis Dealy and I from *The Challenger Sale*, https://repeatablesuccess.com/2013/01/19/challenger-sale-reframe-exercise/.

RETRACING FOOTSTEPS: SAMPLE STEP 5 REVISIONS

Step 5: Planning, Assessing, and Testing the Solution

Example Topic Challenge: Cogito Ergo Sum: *How can cognitive technologies transform the way financial institutions deal with the impact of regulatory change on their consumer lending documentation?*

After conducting a pre-mortem, receiving feedback during the Milestone Meeting and Shadow Team Meeting about the real-world potential, limitations, and functionality of the solution, the team realized that banks—not just consumers—can suffer unjustly under the current regulatory system. This is because banks experience reputational and financial harm due to an inability to systematically and swiftly prove compliance with financial regulations. They also realized that their solution was a bit one-sided, focusing only on training the consumer, which was a benefit to the consumer and could potentially decrease the number of complaints lodged (which was a benefit to the bank). Further, they realized that their solution had value beyond just the one banking client.

- This tool should be an auditable system that enables banks to educate and train consumers on the terms and conditions of their lending documentation—and track the consumers' progress in completing that education. This will enable banks to answer to the Ombudsman and prove compliance in a swifter, more systematic way.
- This tool could be replicated and rolled out to other financial institutions or firms, thus providing a revenue-generating opportunity for the creating entity.

A-Brand-and-Solution-in-a-Sentence-or-2 Revised: Clear Loan is an online training tool to help banks reduce consumer-borrower complaints and more efficiently prove compliance with financial regulations when consumer-borrowers complain by: (1) providing a training platform to educate consumer-borrowers on the terms and conditions of their lending documentation; and (2) assisting banks in providing standardized evidence of compliance by auditing consumers' completion and understanding of lending documentation training so that banks can avoid needless fines.

Week 10: Goals, Content, Coach Session 1, and Optional Expert Meeting Overview (Steps 1–5)

The main goal for the week is for the team to begin putting together its business plan. This is why there is a webinar on the topic and also lots of different reading and resources to help the team get started. The deliverables will look intense however, the team can also work on these during week 11. Remember, as noted above, at this point the team has already done a lot of work that is part of a traditional business plan. For example, the team has already identified the key "customer/user" target audience and learned a lot about them. Team members have done a lot of research on the market need and size along with the competition. Now they need to turn to some financials, that is, how much will it cost to produce and deliver the product or service? What are the start-up costs and initial investment needs (and what will the funds be used for)? How much does it cost (time and resources) to reach, acquire, support, and retain the target audience? How will the product or service be priced? What is the projected return on the investment and by what year might the venture be profitable?

In addition to business planning, it is important that the team continue in Step 4, that is, flushing out their solution and developing their prototype as well as refining their problem and understanding of the target audience (Steps 2–3).

To accomplish both goals, this week the team should meet with their Coach—preferably at the same time or on the same day that they usually meet with the PM (and in lieu of the PM Meeting; but, of course, the PM may join in). They should prepare a presentation that includes Steps 1–5 (in whatever order is most compelling, which is usually not in order) to receive questions and feedback from the Coach. Also, they should either meet with an External Expert (e.g., Business Planning or Tech Expert) or some other people external to the team for an outsider and fresh point of view and to begin practicing pitching.

At some point (either during one of the meetings or via email or chat), the PM should remind the teams of their upcoming deliverables for week 11 which is to continue to flush out their solution and prototype and business plans. Next week, the teams will present their Projects of Worth (including a deck of no more than 20 slides) in approximately 10-15 minutes to their Shadow Teams and to the Lead Facilitator during Milestone Meeting 4 for feedback so there is prep work to do for those meetings as well.

Week 11: Goals, Content, and Milestone Meeting 4 Overview (Steps 1–5 Focusing on Steps 4–5)

The main goals for week 11 are for teams to further develop their business plans and prototypes and determine a creative way that they will bring the consumer story to life at the final ConPosium (Steps 4–5). The latter is important because creating a video or animation to bring the consumer stories to life can be very time consuming. This is also true of building a prototype. I have witnessed "live demos" of prototypes fail too many times. Either the tech does not work at the moment or the person goes off script and takes too much of the presentation time. Demos of prototypes are best when prerecorded and shared in a way that leaves nothing to chance. So part of refining prototypes this week is also beginning to create the mock website or app or video of the product or process to show how the product or process works from the target audiences' points of view.

During the Milestone Meeting, the team should present a slide deck of no more than 20 slides that includes their narrow *Problem Plane* statement, why and how the problem is important (supported by research, stats, and data), a set of consumer/user stories that illustrates the narrow problem, description of the *Brand-and-a-Solution-in-a-Sentence-or-2*, and a demonstration of the prototype along with a business plan. Note: Teams should NOT put the slides together in order of the 5 Steps. Instead, they should put them together in the most persuasive way! I always find that beginning with the consumer story or some hard and fast POW! facts supporting the importance of the problem/need/opportunity is the best way to start. However, teams should have creative license to start how they want.

Before having the team present their progress, this might be a good time to do a teaming exercise. The last few weeks have been very intense for the team and they have not met with the PM or the Lead Facilitator in a while, so consider doing one of the teaming exercises included in the Appendix that not only helps the team feel good, but also has a little substance to it, such as *The Tools' Tools Teaming Exercise*, which has a focus on sharing tools the individual members of the team feel are most effective for business planning or prototyping. This helps the team "team" and share knowledge. Given that, by this point, the teams should have pitched their problem and solution many times, this is an appropriate time to give feedback on presentation format, order, and style—including deck layout and design. This is also a good time to make suggestions on how the team can make their problem and consumer stories more compelling. Additionally, it is time to point out areas they can cut from their presentation—especially as eventually teams have to cull the presentations down to 5 minutes. Of course, the business plans will need a lot of attention and critique. The hope is that there is time to begin exploring some branding elements with the team (Step 4). Consider beginning a discussion about branding by doing the *My Favorite Brand Exercise* as this will be great prep for the week to come, which focuses on branding. Then, their answers to this exercise can help begin discussions about the branding elements of the team's project (name, tagline, logo, deck look and feel). Also, the teams met with their Shadow Teams this week as well, so the Lead Facilitator should probe any learnings from there—or if the Shadow Meetings are yet to come this week, identify what they should focus the Shadow Team on in terms of feedback. Then, as always, the meeting should conclude with a review of the deliverables which include attending or watching a webinar about branding and marketing, working on *The Brand Matrix Exercise*, prototyping, business planning, an optional meeting with a Branding or Tech Engineering Expert.

Week 12: Goals, Content, Optional Expert Meeting, and PM Team Meeting Overview (Steps 1–5)

While continuing to develop their prototypes, consumer story depictions, and business plans, the main goal for the week is for the teams to learn about branding and how it is different from marketing and to begin developing a brand for their Projects of Worth. This is why we suggest an optional meeting with an external expert on branding. That said, if you have an internal expert on branding who can help, by all means have the team pitch to them as well!

Although the PM hopefully attended either the Shadow Team Meeting last week and/or the Milestone Meeting, the PM hasn't led a meeting with the team in quite some time (since week 8), so the PM might start with some kind of check-in exercise to see how the team is feeling about *The Brand Matrix Exercise* that they were assigned to work on prior to the meeting. A good one for that is the *Rose-Cactus-Rocket Ship Exercise*, wherein each person shares their rose (what is going great), their cactus (what's prickling them), and their rocket ship (where they want to go). Another one that I made up and works wonders super quick is: *The Temperature Take Exercise* wherein you ask people to close their eyes and shout out whether they feel like Happy Bananas, Peaceful Palms, or Rotten Tomatoes. And since the team will be meeting virtually, everyone should first shut their video off and turn their microphones on. Then, on the count of three, they can shout out their choice. If there are any Rotten Tomatoes they will be sure to be heard and it is a sign to tread lightly during the meeting and to explore the disconnects and help the team reach consensus.

Have the team present a short pitch describing the problem and solution/prototype, including what they have so far on their business plan, brand, and tagline. At this point, the PM should feel free to comment on any parts of the pitch but be sure to save time to go through their work on the *Brand Matrix* and conduct some exploration into the brand name and tagline they created so the team can build on it and enhance it. As for deliverables for the coming week. importantly, we are nearing the end of the journey, so teams should begin working on their presentation materials. If they didn't present a consumer story video or animation, they should be pushed to begin creating it. If they couldn't succinctly talk through the key components of the business plan, they should be pushed to do so (saving the detail for the appendix of their decks). It is important that in this next week, the team reviews past Projects of Worth presentations, decks, and business plans so they are clear on what they need to create. At this point, they should be thinking as well about their commercials. Teams should be urged to create storyboards of their ideas for the commercial.

The good news is that this next week's webinar will be focused on how to put together a dynamic pitch, the art of storytelling, scripting, and powerful presenting, all of which will help with their upcoming deliverables which include further developing all aspects of their Projects of Worth and the materials for the final presentations. Also, teams need to prepare a 10-15 minutes presentation (and script) for the upcoming Coach Session 2, again not in order of the 5 Steps but instead in the order that is most compelling. And they should be reminded that this coaching session is in lieu of a PM Team Meeting and the last scheduled coaching session so they should make the most of it.

Week 13: Goals, Content, and Coach Session 2 Overview (Steps 1–5)
The main goal for week 13 is for teams to begin developing how they will present their Projects of Worth at the ConPosium. Each team should have a new script that can be presented during the meeting with the Coach. The teams should not worry about having a beautiful deck that matches the script *yet* but, of course, it would be ideal if they had

some slides to go along with the script because this will help the Coach better understand the script. The goal is a compelling script that describes the problem in a moving way supported with research (data and facts), brings to life the consumer/user target audience experiencing the problem, shares a prototype that demonstrates how the solution works, and contains a business plan. It would be ideal if the team had a creative way to bring the consumer story to life already developed. And it would be even cooler if they had a first draft of their commercial.

Although it might be tempting for the Coach to stay silent and let the team present the entire script without interruption, that will likely do a disservice to the team. First, the Coach can't take notes fast enough and also listen at the same time. So it may be better if the Coach stops the team the moment they are confused or have a question. Second, it is a learning experience for the team to hear how what they say resonates—or does not resonate. They also learn if they communicate what they intend to, so interruptions in the moment are essential for that. Third, in real life, except in very formal presentations, we are often interrupted and have to explain ourselves. So my advice is to have the Coach interrupt away! And since there is no PM meeting this week, the PM must be sure to either attend the Coach session or send an email or chat to the teams to cover deliverables for the week and remind the teams that the Milestone Meeting 5 (Mock Presentations) are next week. They should treat these mocks as real rehearsals and present without stopping and with a beautifully designed deck. To help the Lead Facilitator, the teams should pre-send any consumer story videos/animations, the draft commercial, the current *Problem Plane* statement, current business plan, their presentation script, and their description of the solution prior to the meeting. Also, if the teams have not yet done so, they should be sure to calendar the various rehearsals that need to be conducted during week 15 with their Coach, PM, and Shadow Team.

Week 14: Goals, Content, and Milestone Meeting 5 Overview (Mock Presentations)

The main goal for the week is for teams to present and receive feedback from the Lead Facilitator on a beautiful, branded slide deck of no more than 20 slides, approximately 5 minutes long if the plan is Ignite-style presentations, but if not then 10-15 minutes long, that includes (but hopefully NOT in this order!) the narrow *Problem Plane* statement, why and how the problem is important (supported by research, i.e., stats and data), the consumer/user stories that illustrate the narrow problem (hopefully brought to life in a moving way), the *Brand-and-Solution-in-a-Sentence-or-2*, brand name, and tagline, a demonstration of the prototype (perhaps a video or mock up), along with a business plan—and an appendix anticipating questions that might be asked and that provides more detailed information than needed for the main presentation. Oh, and also the team's commercial!

Again I repeat on purpose: Teams should NOT put the slides together in order of the 5 Steps. Instead, they should put them together in the most persuasive way, taking into account all that they have learned about deck development, scripting, and storytelling. The feedback that the teams need is not only on the presentation as a whole but also on the deck, script, the tone, the timing, and the flow. Everything, big to small, even as small as that all decks should have page numbers; how can judges refer to the presentation without page numbers? Or that the font size should be 35 or higher; how can the audience read the slides if the font is too small? Additionally, individual team members need feedback on their presentation style, including mannerisms, presence, ticks (like "umms" and "you knows"), stance, eye contact, speed/pace, and intonation.

During this final Milestone Meeting, the Lead Facilitator should let the team present once in its entirety before giving feedback. It is a MOCK after all. Prior to beginning, they should tell the presenters that they are taking notes. Beware of facial expressions during the presentation so as to not provide any confusing or off-putting cues. Then the Lead Facilitator should provide overarching feedback. I recommend using the *W3 TALA* or *I Like, I Wish, I Wonder* feedback exercises discussed earlier. Then the team should present again, only this time the Lead Facilitator should interrupt at key places to point out when things REALLY resonate or when there is confusion. After each person presents, the Facilitator should take the time to tell that individual presenter what they do well and what they need to work on. There is likely no need to remind teams of their deliverables for the next week as it is rehearsal week and all will be well aware!

Week 15: Goals, Content, and Rehearsals Overview

The main goal for the week prior to the ConPosium is to rehearse, receive feedback, and revise and refine. The rehearsals should be fun; however, they need to be run like "real" presentations with no interruptions or "let me start over" or "scratch that." Also, preferably the rehearsals should be done in the same space/place that the real presentations will occur. So, if teams will present on a certain virtual platform, that is where rehearsals should happen. If they will be in-person, ideally, they should happen in-person and preferably on the stage that it will happen for real and with the same tech devices—microphones, presentation slide clickers, etc. If microphones are not available, we recommend holding a different object (banana or fake microphone which can easily and cheaply be purchased on the internet) or wearing a headset (if they will have a lapel microphone) because handoffs of microphones and presentation slide clickers can be a very tricky thing in real time. Even in a virtual world, "handoffs" can be tricky, because people forget to turn their microphones on/off and sometimes there is internet delay. So practice, practice, practice.

These rehearsals and the practice Q&A should be timed exactly to what will occur at the ConPosium—which will vary depending on whether teams are presenting Ignite-style (or some other longer format) and how many judges will be included and how long judges can speak/ask questions. The *Rehearsals Dos and Don'ts & Q&A Tips Resource* is a great tool to set the rehearsals up for success.

Also, this week it is key to perfect the choreography of the entire presentation, whether it is virtual or in-person. Every team member needs to know exactly how things will flow and who will speak when, who will fill in for whom if someone is absent or freezes (literally virtually or figuratively on stage), who is handling the tech, and what will be done if the tech doesn't work entirely. What if the team's video doesn't play? They should have a plan, for example, a skit or one person ready to describe what they would be seeing. Even though we have materials turned in one to two days in advance to check the tech and make sure all components "work," things still go wrong on the big day. Believe me, we have had tech fail not only in virtual presentations but also during in-person presentations where we have lost complete sound and Wi-Fi. The point is: the team needs to have a contingency plan in place. This is also true for individuals. We have the teams assign understudies to each team member so that if a team member freaks out on stage and cannot recall their script or is sick and cannot attend, another team member can easily fill in.

The Coaches, Shadow Teams, and PMs should definitely review the run-of-show the Lead Facilitator creates for the ConPosium and also the *Rehearsals Dos and Don'ts & Q&A Tips Resource* before these rehearsals because they provide tips on how best to run the rehearsals and what to provide feedback on for the participants. (They also provide tips to the participants on how best to answer the judges' questions, so be on the lookout for how and what to critique.)

Last, don't forget that stress runs high the week prior to the ConPosium. So, while it might be tempting to jump right into rehearsals, take the time to do a teaming exercise to ensure the team is acting as one and feeling as one. A teaming exercise that I made up that ties to the goals for the week works well here. It is called *Superhero Presentation Power Tricks Exercise*. The goal of this exercise is for team members to share their own personal superhero presentation power tricks, that is, what each individual does immediately before a presentation to rev themselves up. For some, it might be a word or phrase we say to ourselves. For others it might be in Madonna-like fashion, striking a pose. So we ask each team member to please share their Superhero Presentation Power Tricks with their team so they can exapt them to source the energy they need to rock this rehearsal and the upcoming ConPosium presentation!

Week 16: ConPosium
(Described in the next chapter.)

CHAPTER **5**

Phase 3: The ConPosium and Beyond

As a recap, the ConPosium is a community-wide event (depending on how you define community) during which the teams present their solutions to a panel of (preferably multidisciplinary) judges who assess, question, and comment on the creativity, viability, and business case of the Project of Worth. It is likely obvious to point out that the ConPosium is hard work because it includes a great deal of reflecting and evaluation. It is a different type of reflection and evaluation than the rehearsals and Milestone Meetings because it is the real thing in front of a much larger group of professionals who are invested in the outcome. Thus everything matters including presentation delivery, the content, look, and feel of the deck, and the individual contributions and stage presence. So, this is also a time for nurturing the self and the team, and it is above all else a time for celebration— celebration of learning and progress and of the community.

Last, although appearing to be the end of the journey, as described earlier, the ConPosium is not the end. It may be for this specific team, but likely not for this project. The ConPosium is as much a part of Step 5 as the business plan is as it is a time for testing and receiving feedback for how to improve the solution (and the pitch). To ensure that it houses both elements (celebration and testing), facilitating the ConPosium requires attention to many details that need to be handled in advance, and perhaps as early as three months in advance.

A. PREPPING FOR THE CONPOSIUM

Like with the Kickoff, there is prep work that needs to be done for the ConPosium because it, too, is a big event in and of itself. In addition to picking a date and securing a format (virtual or in-person) and a platform or location, there is more that should be done (and decisions to be made) to help the ConPosium be a success, including (1) Creating the Right Space and Place; (2) Selecting Judges and the MC (Master of Ceremonies);

(3) Identifying the Assessment Criteria and Process; and (4) Marketing the Event (internally and externally; before and after the ConPosium).

1. Creating the Right Space and Place (12 to 2 Weeks Prior to the ConPosium): It is important to consider the space and mood for the ConPosium just as with the Kick-Off. There is nothing worse than having an energized team deflated by a boring, snoring, unexciting event space in which to present ideas they have worked so hard on. Music and the type of seating can greatly enhance the energy of the space. Consider including some couches and chairs and also some decorations that inspire and create the right mood, for example, palm trees for relaxing, or black curtains and white tablecloths and lights for a formal tuxedo celebratory mood, or balloons to create cheer. Also consider wall dec-orations to match the theme and that look great behind the presenters for photographs and future social media marketing opportunities. If there was a theme at the KickOff, the ConPosium should continue that theme. For example, if the theme was about climbing a mountain (and the song for the KickOff lip sync was "Ain't No Mountain High Enough"), the decorations, wall art, and song at ConPosium could be themed around reaching the summit. (Think "Rocky Mountain High.") Or if the theme was based on reaching a new galaxy or outer space (and the KickOff lip sync song was "Welcome to the Space Jam"), the decorations, wall art, and song at ConPosium could be about reaching the moon. (Think "Moondance" or "Dancing in the Moonlight.") And, as with the Kickoff, consider what swag you might give away at the event to create community and camaraderie and reinforce the theme. If this is to be an ongoing program that new people at your company or firm participate in, think long term. Pins are great swag items that can keep a theme year to year but also change to denote another year.

The layout of the room, if the event is in-person, is also essential. It is imperative that there is a stage. Ideally, it should be above ground level. Do away with podiums because presentations should be without notes of course! Confidence monitors are essential so pre-senters do not have to turn their backs to see what is on the screen. And a big floor timer that can be easily seen from the stage does wonders not just for the presenters but especially for the judges to keep them on time (more on that later!). Also, consider how you will place the judges. People want to see the judges' faces when they ask questions, but the judges need to see the presentations. The way we handle this in LawWithoutWalls is that we have a second camera and a second screen that shows the judges' faces even though their backs are to the audience—like on the TV show *The Voice*. Note: We also have a second timer that the judges can see! Keeping judges on time is sometimes the hardest part.

Some consideration should also be given to the length of the event, the audience's band-width, and the level of interactiveness. If you have a lot of presentations, the length of the presentations matter. Generally, pitches should not be more than 15 minutes in length (with 5 to 10 minutes of Q&A) and, as you now know, I'm a big believer in 5 minute presentations in Ignite-style, that is, 20 self-moving slides in 5 minutes with 5 to 10 minutes of Q&A from with expert judges. In addition to length, consider how you will space the presentations to keep the level of engagement high but also ensure fairness so that those that go last are not least. When do you serve food and drinks and provide those organic networking and community-building opportunities that are as important at the ConPosium as at the Kick-Off? Importantly, if there are more than three teams, how do you keep the audience engaged during the presentations if there are many back-to-back? One way we do that is through a live chat that we show on an alternate screen that all participants have access to. This is a great way for coaches and other people who have helped the teams along the way (but who are not on stage) to support the team as they present. They can provide links with more data in support of the problem. They can provide answers to the judges' questions that build on what the team says out loud in the moment. And the rest of the audience can provide positive feedback and questions for future thought. We always keep the entire transcript to share with the teams so that they can use this to improve their solutions and pitches on a go-forward. Of course, it's important to set the rules of engagement for these chats, that is, the last thing we need is negativity in a live chat featured on a screen in the room.

We also have yet another screen where we display Twitter. As noted below in the marketing section, we create a Twitter handle for the event and urge our community to tweet as the ConPosium flows; and we post the tweets as they happen. (Of course, if this is an internal confidential event, this wouldn't be appropriate.) We also have a live stream of the event for viewers who cannot attend in-person. Therefore, the correct stage and screen placement is critical to ensure that viewers on the live stream are seeing the screens and the presenters and that the space/place in the virtual world is also well done. Not an easy feat! Moreover, all of this tech (screens, confidence monitors, timers, cameras, microphones (lapels and handhelds)) needs to be decided in advance and sometimes ordered from external companies if your organization does not have all the equipment needed.

Another key question to address is, how do you keep the audience engaged AND seated during transition times between presentations? Remember, there are always transition times between presentations especially if in-person, because you have to pull up the right presentation deck and people need to be outfitted with lavalier microphones. To that end, music can fill the void and keep people in their seats. In LawWithoutWalls, we ask the teams to pick a theme song that they want played as they "set up" during this transition time. It helps create an exciting vibe and keeps the audience in their seats, and at the same time, it helps the teams get in the right mood, that is, jazzed up or calmed down, depending on their music preference. And it helps the live-stream attendees stay engaged too!

All of this is also important if you are holding a virtual ConPosium—maybe even more. Music during segues can do wonders for energy and awkwardness. Using a platform wherein you can control what the viewers see and what they can do is also recommended (vs basic Zoom wherein the audience can change the settings for themselves). And as with the in-person event, if there is a live chat enabled, there needs to be a person that is helping steer it to ensure it is positive and engaging and not distracting.

2. Selecting Judges and the MC (8 to 4 weeks prior to the ConPosium): Let's start with the MC first. It is important to pick your MC carefully. MCs actually have a lot of power in terms of setting the tone of the event, keeping people engaged, and timing. If they don't keep time, they can blow up the whole plan! Also, MCs who read bios from notes are Debbie downers. Pick someone who can memorize and highlight people's accomplishments in a genuine way and who can say something substantive (and maybe even funny) during those transition times mentioned above, for example, after each presentation, before the judges are announced and ask questions, etc. And, as is always true, the expectations that aren't set aren't met. So be sure to share your expectations with your chosen MC and vet that person somehow so you don't pick someone that goes rogue. I like to give this task to junior people on the team or in the community as a way of empowering them. However, when I do that, we rehearse their introductions and they receive the same type of nit-picky feedback the teams do during rehearsals in terms of verbal ticks, body posture, hand gestures, movement, and so on.

Now, on to the judges. Judges need to be selected and invited at least one month prior to the event, even better if two months prior to the event as participants need to know who they will be judged by. Arguably, it would be even better if they knew this prior to committing to the journey. For example, if the judges will be clients, this can be a real motivator for a group of professional service providers. The same is true if the judges are senior people from elite companies or successful entrepreneurs or venture capitalists.

However, who they are is less important than how they behave and how they will contribute. No matter who you pick, don't assume they know how to be a judge. Don't assume they know how to give feedback in keeping with the culture of your company or firm. Don't assume they know how to ask questions that are appropriate in tone and scope and don't assume they will show up on time and/or stay within the time limits you set. So, spend the time up front on training and prepping them on how to judge. In fact, the judges who will attend need to be prepped, even more than you think. They need to be told not only when they are judging but what time they should arrive. They need to be told what type of feedback is appropriate and what types of questions are NOT ok. They need to be told what their time limits are and how they will be handled if they go over the time limit. And in addition to that, they need to be vetted. I have made this mistake before. Just because someone is the general counsel or CEO of a Fortune 500 company does not mean they know how to hear a pitch and, in the moment, ask inquisitive, important questions and provide constructive (nonoffensive) feedback. The judges also need training on the tech and the flow of your event. It can be extremely annoying when judges repeatedly tap the microphone to see if it is working before they provide feedback or when they shut the microphone off when they hand it to the next judge, or when they go on and on and on even after the timer has run. Frustrating!! The goal is for the ConPosium to feel like a Pitch Event and not some second-class scene from the TV show *The Office*. To help with all of this, I create Judge's Instructions that lay it all out. I also ensure that they can see the timer (and so can the audience) so that they are "shamed" into stopping on time.

Also, consider how many judges make sense from a substantive and efficient standpoint. Having more judges can be better for diversity, but that also requires more time in training and more time at the event for introductions, feedback, and transitions. Also, rotating judges after each team or a group of teams impacts voting equality but can help substantive quality. If you have different judges for each presentation, you can ensure that each of the judges has some expertise in the topic. But this makes voting and selection of winners complicated (as discussed more below).

3. Identifying the Assessment Criteria and Process (8 to 4 weeks prior to the Con-Posium): Whether you are picking a winner or not, some consideration has to be paid to what criteria will be used for assessment and who will do the assessing. We always like to give instructions to our judges to give feedback on the following criteria: viability of the solution (which includes the business plan), creativity of the solution (which includes the branding and prototyping), and the presentation itself (which includes the deck and communication style and flow). If you are picking winners, then the question is what will be the categories for the winners? They could be the same as the assessment criteria. However, instead, you might consider: Best Overall, Best Business Case, Best Branding, Best Presentation (deck/style). It doesn't really matter what you choose but that you choose ahead of time and are super-transparent about it! In fact, an argument could be made that participants should know starting in week 1 how their projects and contributions will be assessed and whether this is a competition. If the ConPosium is a competition with a winner and you are doing so by some kind of vote, it is imperative that a lot of thought is done PRIOR to the event as to how the voting will happen. And it is important that you tell the participants how the voting will work and what role the judges play. Fairness is a big deal here and shouldn't be underrated. And voting is complicated when you have multiple teams and when you have different sets of judges for different teams. In Law-WithoutWalls, we often have a totally different set of three to four judges for each team who provide feedback and ask questions. They generally do not stay for the entire set of presentations. So, the way we handle voting is that we have a hand-selected group of people who are the *official silent voting judges* who watch ALL the presentations and vote, but they do not provide feedback or questions. The judges who ask questions and provide feedback are not allowed to vote (unless they are there for every presentation). However, regardless of the talking, judges help the teams improve their projects and pitches and they also serve to "sway" the audience because we always have an "audience choice" winner in addition to the winners selected by the official voting judges.

Another question to consider is, when should voting occur? If you have 16 presentations, how will the judges (and the community if you are having an audience vote) remember by the end? If you vote after each presentation, how will people be able to vote accurately on the first few without having anything to compare to? And if the presentations occur over more than one day, how can you rely on an audience vote when some people might not attend all the presentations? Of course, all these questions are made simpler by the fewer number of teams, but once there are more than five teams, they become critical to answer in advance.

Also, there is a lot to consider in deciding *how* people cast votes. If you are going to use a survey tool, like Google Forms, how do you ensure that people do not vote twice? How do you make sure that the Google Form captures the right responses and adds them up electronically in a format that is easy to use and understand? This may seem simple, but I have seen it messed up multiple times. Also, when will you announce the winners? If right then and there at the event (which is what most people prefer), what will the audience do while you tally? Just sit there? In LawWithoutWalls, we either play some videos (that we created over the course of the journey) to keep them involved and engaged as we tally, or we host a cocktail event and they celebrate while we tally. Another question to consider is: How will you announce? Typing up slides at the last minute is a nightmare. We always have pre-prepared winner slides of *all* the teams so we can quickly choose the winners and not have to type it up last minute. Lastly, what do the winners receive? A trophy? Funding or commitment to move the project forward? If the latter, this might be a great sponsorship opportunity for the company or firm to consider.

4. Marketing The Event (4 weeks prior to 2 weeks after the ConPosium): A lot of page space was dedicated to the subject of the importance of marketing in *Leader Upheaval*, so I won't go into detail here. Suffice it to say that thought needs to be put into how and when you message about the ConPosium. The marketing plan should not only be directed to people you will invite to attend in-person (or virtually or via live stream) but also others inside the company or firm to raise awareness about the progress that has ensued, that is, if there is a ConPosium, this means solutions have been created (remember the Progress Principle!). Additionally, the marketing plan should include target audiences and stakeholders external to the company (e.g., clients, potential clients, potential sponsors, and even perhaps, competitors). Running a collaborative, innovation journey sets your firm apart and sends a message about your goals, values, and culture. The ConPosium is a great way to "brag" without tooting the department's or company's horn. It's also a great way to enhance the diversity of your audience that attends the event from inside and external to your company or firm.

5. Laying the Leg Work for Continued Community Building (4 weeks prior and into infinity): The teams and their Shadow Teams will need no help bonding. However, like with the KickOff, it is important that you preplan how to bake in community building during the event. We do this in a few ways. First, we play the original lip sync that we played at KickOff. Second, we create a second lip sync for the ConPosium (also on theme of course!). You will be surprised how many more people are willing to partake now that they saw the first lip sync. This, however, takes planning and needs to be done a few weeks prior to the ConPosium. Another way to build community is to have some helpers photograph and film participants over the course of the ConPosium and then splice it together during the ConPosium so that it can be played at the end. We usually pick uplifting music in line with our theme and play this while we are tallying votes. Showcasing people in the audience is a great way to keep people in their seats. And the video quality doesn't have to be perfect (and can be edited later for a better version). Of course, community building should not stop with the ConPosium, especially if you have a new cohort of teams starting a journey in the future or if you are continuing to work on bringing some of the projects to life. So community building continues into infinity or until you stop doing innovation journeys which arguably should be never (given the pace at which the world is changing technologically). In other words, it is never too early to start planning your next PopUp (highlighted in Chapter 2 as a key community builder).

B.   FACILITATING THE CONPOSIUM

So it is week 16, now what? What needs to be done 1 to 3 days before the ConPosium starts?

Presentation Materials Due Date and Review of Materials: We always require teams to provide their slide decks and all materials embedded within them (e.g., videos, audio files, etc.) at least 24 hours prior to the ConPosium and often 48 hours when we have more than 10 teams (which we always do in LawWithoutWalls but that is not necessarily true when facilitating journeys with firms). The reason for the lead time is to provide time for us to review the decks for errors, especially errors related to animations within the deck (timed or otherwise) and video/audio playback. (We also invariably find typos and graphical errors, i.e., something is cut off from the slide or doesn't pop up when clicked.) Checking the slides for the teams and reverting back to them to receive the corrected files and slides is a service that some might say should be left to the teams. However, as mentioned above, the point of the ConPosium is not just to "teach" the teams lessons on presenting and pitching but also for them to receive real feedback for forward improvement AND for celebration. No one feels good about a presentation flop because the tech inside the deck didn't work. That's definitely not very celebratory. Plus it is an incompetent failure that could have been avoided. Second, if the deck doesn't work, the team loses time and is often ruffled and so the pitch is not only incomplete but also extremely rocky which inhibits the ability of the team to learn and gain insights on how to improve their projects. So we take care of our teams this way. It is tedious and detail oriented but it helps make the ConPosium a success not only for the teams but for the leaders too. Our reputation is also on the line for how the ConPosium goes and how the teams present. So, it may be hand-holding but it is worth it from every angle.

Tech Tests and Set-Up One Day Prior: The only way to ensure the tech goes smoothly during the event is to test it a day prior and not the day of the event. If you have spent the time to create the right space and place, ordered extra screens so that the judges' faces can be shown as they give feedback, and so the community can chat and see their

Tweets, and created a live-stream platform, then you should most definitely take the time to check the tech the day prior. Why a full day prior? Often when big tech (screens, long cable lines) fails it is not something that can be fixed on the spot, and it may require a reconfiguration of the layout of the venue. We have a full day with our tech people to do run-throughs to plan for any possible mishap like the Wi-Fi going down, the microphones losing sound, and so on. In the last 14 years, all of this has happened. We also rehearse transitions between decks so that the AV people understand the timing and flow and what needs to be pulled up when and to which screens. Additionally, we map out how microphones and clickers will be provided to teams during transition times and who is responsible for each. Last, we run through every team's deck and recheck all the video and audio files one final time (on the main screen) to ensure they work and that the AV folks know how to help if there is a glitch, that is, if sound is lower on one recording than another, etc. All of this is extremely tedious, but it helps ensure the ConPosium fulfills its goals of being a testing ground for the viability of the projects and a celebration. And although less has to be done for a virtual event, a day prior tech rehearsal is essential in that situation too. And assigning roles to helpers is almost more important with a virtual event. Problems rarely occur because there are not enough people. In addition to Tech setup and testing, the room itself needs to be set up (decorated to the theme), the swag put where it is supposed to go, the seating set up the way it is intended. All of this should be done the day prior. If something is missing or broken, there is time to find a replacement.

Helper Rehearsals: For any big event to occur without a hitch, there need to be helper rehearsals that identify specific people for certain jobs. And I'm a big fan of assigning roles to ONE person. That one person can transition during the event. But problems rarely occur because there are not enough people assigned to a role but instead because too many are assigned and no one person feels responsible or no one was assigned. Instead, hiccups happen due to lack of clarity about who is supposed to do what, that is, who is in charge of handing out nametags in an orderly fashion? (When 200 people are standing in line, that's a problem!) Who is in charge of ensuring each judge has a bottle of water and a clean notepad? Who is in charge of putting the correct judges' name cards on the judging table for each transition? Who is in charge of ensuring the microphones are *on* at the judging table (because participants often shut them off for some reason)? Who is running the timer? Who is holding up timer cards? Who is in charge of ringing the bell (or the xylophone) to communicate when it is time for people to return? The list goes on. And the list needs to be made prior to the event and reviewed the day prior. This is also true for a virtual event. Who is in charge of running the chat? Who is in charge of inserting links as requested by the team? Who is in charge of tracking questions put in the chat? Who is playing music during transitions? Who is the back-up screen sharer if someone's screen share is interrupted? The list goes on in the virtual world as well.

Going with the Flow: If you have done all that is outlined above, it is time now to leave it to the event gods and go with the flow. Remember, the participants do not know the actual run-of-show. They do not know exactly what you planned and how you planned it.

So if something goes wrong, that is, a judge doesn't show up, a video doesn't play, the coffee runs out, if you go with the flow, everyone will follow. I will share one last story with you to bring this to life. At a recent ConPosium event where we had 12 teams presenting and we were in the middle of the sixth team's presentation, we lost all Wi-Fi and sound. Microphones didn't work. PowerPoints didn't work. The lights were on and everyone was waiting. What do you do in a situation like that? Well, what we did is, we sang. During our KickOff, we had conducted the *Silver and Gold Exercise* that includes singing the old children's nursery rhyme adage: *Make New Friends but Keep the Old, One Is Silver and the Other Gold*. Its purpose is to serve as an icebreaker to get people to introduce one of their "old" LawWithoutWalls friends to one of their new ones. So, when we lost all sound and Wi-Fi at the ConPosium? I shouted out: "Let's Sing." And started singing the *Make New Friends* song and you know what? Everyone followed. And it made the time go by and when we were up and ready again, the community was engaged and warm and felt safe. Everyone knew that nothing could go wrong if we could get past no Wi-Fi and no sound.

Conclusion

It's tough to close a book that is designed for continual re-reading. To that end, my hope is that you never read this conclusion and instead that you have used this book as it was designed, that is, to help you lead your own change efforts. My hope is also that you are reading this conclusion because you have actually tried your hand at implementing The 3-4-5 Method™ and found it to be as easy as 3-4-5. I also hope at this point you have reaped its true rewards. In other words, I hope that in addition to successfully reaching a solution to a challenge, or leveraging an important opportunity, you have seen (with your own eyes) a change in the mindsets, skillsets, and behaviors of professionals who went on the journey with you. Also, I hope this book has helped you in your own personal journey to grow as a leader and a manager of change and culture creation because, after all, as we learned in *Leader Upheaval*, "it is the journey that matters, in the end."[1]

---

[1] URSULA K. LE GUIN, THE LEFT HAND OF DARKNESS 200 (New York: Ace Books, 2000).

Appendix

A. LIST OF FIGURES

Figure 1.1	The Professional Skills Delta outlining the three levels of skills/attributes needed for professional service providers to provide client-centric service
Figure 1.2	A chart depicting the 3 Phases in The 3-4-5 Method™
Figure 2.1	A sample calendar for a 4-month journey utilizing The 3-4-5 Method™
Figure 2.2	The winning entry of a British multinational consumer goods company's internal competition to join a team on a 4-month journey in LawWithoutWalls
Figure 2.3	A chart detailing one option for team makeup
Figure 2.4	A chart detailing team makeup from a Microsoft program led by Michele DeStefano
Figure 3.1	A chart providing a general run-of-show timeline for a 1-day KickOff
Figure 4.1	A sample weekly calendar for a 4-month journey utilizing The 3-4-5 Method™

B. SAMPLE 4-WEEK AND 3-DAY JOURNEY SCHEDULES

Sample 4-Week Journey Schedule

WK	CONTENT
1	KickOff and Step 1
2	Steps 2 and 3
3	Steps 4 and 5 (and revise Steps 2 and 3 as needed)
4	Steps 4 and 5 (including deck and commercial development)
	Rehearsals and ConPosium

Sample 3-Day Journey Schedule

DAY	AM/PM	CONTENT
1	AM PM	KickOff Steps 1 and 2
2	AM PM	Steps 2 and 3 Steps 4 and 5 (and revise Steps 2 and 3 as needed)
3	AM PM	Steps 4 and 5 (including deck and commercial development) Rehearsals and ConPosium

C. LIST OF THE 3-4-5 METHOD™ EXERCISES AND RESOURCES (INSTRUCTIONS AVAILABLE AT MICHELEDESTEFANO.COM OR MOVELAW.COM)

#	EXERCISE OR RESOURCE	PURPOSE	TIMING
1	*Barriers Preventing Collaboration Exercise*	To identify barriers that are preventing the team from collaborating and to enhance teaming	KickOff
2	*Best-Worst and What-I-Learned Exercise*	To elicit thoughts and learnings about the content that was assigned or to share best and worst teaming experiences to enhance teaming	Steps 1–5 (especially after a webinar or assigned reading)
3	*Childhood Stories Exercise*	To enhance teaming and channel our inner 7-year-old, creative selves	KickOff Steps 3 and 5
4	*Delta-Skills Vision Exercise*	To practice self-awareness, commit to honing new skills, and share with teammates the value you bring to the team	KickOff
5	*Doctor Know It All*[1]	To practice the Three Rules of Engagement, improve listening skills, and enhance teaming and ideating	KickOff Steps 1–5 ConPosium (especially before presenting)
6	*Find Your Partner Exercise*	To enhance networking and community building	KickOff PopUp
7	*Getting on the Same Purpose Plane Exercise*	To get the team on the same "plane" as it relates to their purpose for going on a collaboration journey	KickOff

---

[1] This exercise is one that is taught in improvisation acting classes. I learned it from Phyllis Dealy.

#	EXERCISE OR RESOURCE	PURPOSE	TIMING
8	*I Like, I Wish, I Wonder Feedback Exercise*	To provide constructive feedback and enhance teaming[2]	KickOff Steps 1–5 After ConPosium
9	*La Tienda Exercise*	To share work style preferences, practice negotiating roles and ideating, and to create a team identity	KickOff
10	*Pancakes or Waffles Exercise*[3]	To enhance teaming and practice consensus building	KickOff Step 1
11	*The Pet-Peeve-Motto Exercise*	To learn about teammates' workstyle preferences, practice listening, and enhance teaming	KickOff Step 1
12	*Quick Mood Check Exercise*	To gauge the energy and happiness of the team	KickOff Steps 1–5 ConPosium
13	*Rose-Cactus-Rocket-Ship Exercise*	To gauge how individuals on the team are feeling about their progress through the 5 Steps	KickOff Steps 1–5
14	*Silver and Gold Exercise*	To enhance networking and community building	Kickoff PopUp
15	*The Band Exercise*	To share work style preferences, practice negotiating roles and ideating, and to create a team identity	KickOff
16	*The Bittersweet Workstyle Exercise*	To build self- and team- awareness of workstyle preferences, share learnings, and enhance teaming	KickOff
17	*The Filling in the Team Holes Exercise*	To enhance understanding of the different workstyle preferences on the team and incentivize flexing and bending	KickOff
18	*The P.A.C.T. Exercise*	To prepare and secure buy-in and commitment from participants for the personal and professional work ahead and agree to a joint team purpose, individual and group accountability, creative cadence, and timing	KickOff

(continued)

---

[2] I learned this feedback tool from Bjarne Tellmann, GC of Haleon.

[3] Renditions of this exercise are widely available on the internet. Anita Ritchie, the Director of LawWithoutWalls, created this version from various sources.

#	EXERCISE OR RESOURCE	PURPOSE	TIMING
19	*The Restaurant Exercise*	To share work style preferences, practice negotiating roles and ideating, and to create a team identity	KickOff
20	*The Start with Why⁴ Exercise*	To enhance networking and community building	KickOff
21	*The Temperature Take Exercise*	To gauge if the team has truly reached consensus	KickOff Steps 1–5
22	*The Tools' Tools Teaming Exercise*	To enhance knowledge sharing and teaming	KickOff Steps 1–5
23	*The Jungle/Animal Kingdom Exercise*	To share work style preferences, practice negotiating roles and ideating, and to create a team identity	KickOff
24	*W3 TALA Feedback Exercise⁵*	To provide constructive feedback and enhance teaming	Any Phase (Any Step)
25	*Hal Gregersen Question Burst Exercise⁶*	To explore the Topic Challenge and find problems and opportunities within	KickOff Step 1
26	*Identifying Topic Areas of Interest Within the Topic Challenge*	To identify areas within the Topic Challenge that have problems ripe for solving and that the team members care about	Step 1
27	*Talent and Topic Expertise Exploration Exercise*	To identify and share team members' respective expertise related to the Topic Challenge and other talents that might help the team on the journey	KickOff Step 1
28	*Butterfly Approach to Convergence Exercise*	To help teams converge anonymously	Steps 1–5
29	*Examples of Problem Trip Maps Resource*	To provide examples of prior project trip maps so that teams understand how to create their maps and the level of detail that is required (and why Step 3 needs to be done before the Trip Map is truly completed)	Steps 2 and 3

---

⁴ I developed this exercise entirely on my own but it was inspired by the book *Start with Why* by Simon Sinek.

⁵ I learned this from Jeff Carr, former GC of Univar.

⁶ Hal Gregersen and Ed Catmull, Prologue to *Questions Are the Answer: A Breakthrough Approach to Your Most Vexing Problems at Work and in Life*, 2018.

#	EXERCISE OR RESOURCE	PURPOSE	TIMING
30	*Getting on the Same Problem Plane Exercise*	To gain consensus on the exact narrow problem the team is solving, who they are solving it for (key target audience(s)), and why solving the problem for these audiences is important	Steps 2 and 3
31	*I Hate It When Exercise*	To mine for gaps and find narrower, solvable problems (pain points) within the Topic Challenge	Step 2
32	*I Just Wish Exercise*	To mine for gaps and opportunities and find narrower, solvable opportunities (hopefuls) within the Topic Challenge	Step 2
33	*Narrower Problem Identification Exercise*	To help guide individual team members' primary and secondary research to find and describe some narrower problems related to the problems the team converged upon earlier	Steps 1 and 2
34	*Problem Convergence: Passion & Practicability Exercise*	To help teams converge on one or two narrow problems in a way that accounts for the level of passion the team has for solving the identified problem and also the problem's solvability	Step 2
35	*Problem Trip Mapping Exercise*	To map the process in which the problem surfaces, chunk the problem down into smaller parts, to begin to identify who is experiencing or being impacted by the problem (and when), and uncover all the various problems within the problem	Steps 2 and 3
36	*Writing Problem Statements Right Exercise*	To learn how to write problem statements with the right level of detail but that do not include a solution within them	Steps 2 and 3
37	*Bringing the Consumer Story to Life Resource*	To view top notch examples of consumer stories brought to life and create inspiration	Steps 3 and 5
38	*Consumer Story Mad Libs® Exercise*[7]	To create consumer/user stories for key target audiences that bring the problem to life from the target audience(s)' point of view	Steps 3 and 2

(continued)

---

[7] I developed this exercise with Erika Pagano, former Director of LawWithoutWalls, current Head of Legal Innovation and Design, Simmons & Simmons.

#	EXERCISE OR RESOURCE	PURPOSE	TIMING
39	*Consumer/ Stakeholder Profile and Problem Refinement Exercise*	To enhance understanding of each target audience(s)' biography, age, occupation, way of living, expertise, level of education etc., and further refine the problem	Steps 3 and 2
40	*CTQ (Critical-to-Quality) Tree Exercise*[8]	To create a diagram that helps translate broad consumer needs into specific, actionable, measurable performance requirements	Step 3
41	*Interviewing Tips and Sample Interview Template Resource*	To guide investigative research of people in the target audience	Steps 1–3
42	*Key Stakeholder Analysis Exercise*	To identify and prioritize all potential stakeholders (internal and external to the company or firm) that may have a stake in, influence over, or be impacted by the problem or the solution	Steps 3 and 2
43	*The 5 Whys and Root Cause Analysis Exercise*[9]	To separate root causes from symptoms, refine problems, and better understand and empathize with the target audience(s)	Steps 3 and 2
44	*A-Brand-and-Solution-in-a-Sentence-or-2 Exercise*	To succinctly describe the branded solution, highlighting its point of difference and benefits and also what it does, for whom, and why	Steps 4 and 5
45	*Applying the "SCAMPER Technique"*[10]	To ideate by (S) Substituting, (C) Combining, (A) Adapting, (M) Modifying, (P) Putting to another use, (E) Eliminating, and (R) Reversing	Step 4
46	*Attribute Ask Exercise*	To ensure that the solution contains the attributes that are expected (based on the problem description) and that are desired (based on the consumer stories)	Step 4

---

[8] Mind Tools Content Team, *Critical to Quality (CTQ) Trees: Translating Broad Customer Needs Into Specific Requirements*, MINDTOOLS, https://www.mindtools.com/pages/article/ctq-trees.htm (last visited July 9, 2022).

[9] Renditions of this exercise are widely available on the internet. I created this version from various sources.

[10] Dr. Fariq Elmansy, *A Guide to the SCAMPER Technique for Creative Thinking*, Designorate.com, April 10, 2015; *see also* SCAMPER Brainstorming Template: https://www.designorate.com/wp-content/uploads/2021/03/DesignorateTemplates_SCAMPER.pdf.

#	EXERCISE OR RESOURCE	PURPOSE	TIMING
47	*Best Idea/Worst Idea Exercise*[11]	To explore how to open our minds to solutions to problems even when those solutions appear on their surface as bad or crazy ideas	Step 4
48	*Brand Matrix Exercise*[12]	To help develop a brand for the solution and identify the solution's physical brand attributes, rational and emotional brand benefits, and the brand image/personality	Step 4
49	*Divergent Wild Idea Generation Exercise*	To ideate without constraints and without critique to begin generating solution possibilities	Step 4
50	*Exploiting Success Exercise*[13]	To conduct convergent ideation by multiplying, dividing, subtracting, or adding	Step 4
51	*Flushing Out the Solution Exercise*	To determine are the key features of the solution, the barriers that need to be overcome for implementation, budget and resources, timing and metrics for success	Steps 4 and 5
52	*Ideating Inside the Box Exaptation Exercise*	To exapt attributes of other phone apps or tech tools that we use and love in order to develop or improve a solution	Step 4
53	*Insight Matrix Exercise*[14]	To help teams engage in "intelligent recombination," that is, to select and combine past successes with new areas/fields	Step 4
54	*MVS Steeple People Exercise*	To ensure the team creates a Minimum Viable Solution that fits like a glove with only the minimum number parts and without unnecessary add-ons (i.e., bells and whistles)	Steps 4 and 5
55	*My Favorite Brand Exercise*[15]	To instigate team thinking about branding and client/consumer centricity	Steps 4

(continued)

---

[11] This exercise is exapted from Tina Seelig, What I Wish I Knew When I Was 20: A Crash Course on Making Your Place in the World 37–39 (2009).

[12] This exercise was developed by Anita Ritchie, Director of LawWithoutWalls.

[13] This exercise is based on learnings from Drew Boyd & Jacob Goldenberg, Inside the Box: A Proven System of Creativity for Breakthrough Results (2014).

[14] I exapted this exercise from these two sources: Ken Favaro with Nadim Yacteen, *The Right Ideas in All the Wrong Places*, Strategy+Business (Mar. 11, 2013), https://www.strategy-business.com/article/cs00007 and William Duggan, Creative Strategy: A Guide for Innovation 40–52 (2013).

[15] This exercise was co-developed with Anita Ritchie, the Director of LawWithoutWalls.

#	EXERCISE OR RESOURCE	PURPOSE	TIMING
56	*Problem and Solution Refinement Exercise*	To gauge whether the solution the team created solves the problem snugly and whether the problem they have identified and presented is clear to listeners of a pitch	Steps 4 and Step 2
57	*Prototyping Examples Resource*	To better understand the various forms a prototype can take e.g., storyboard, mock website, wireframe, mockup of how the app/product will work and be used by the user/consumer	Step 4
58	*Random Objects Association Exercise*	To associate and add to ideation by including attributes of random objects	Step 4
59	*Scene-by-Scene Flowchart Prototyping Exercise*	To begin the prototyping process	Step 4
60	*User Journey Mapping Examples and Tools Resource*	To help teams create a consumer journey map that visualizes exactly how the user will interface with the solution and how the solution will work step by step	Steps 4 and 3
61	*What I Love Most Exercise*	To help refine/further develop the solution and prototype, and start thinking about branding	Step 4
62	*Business Planning Checklist Resource*	To ensure all components of the business plan are included	Step 5
63	*Business Planning SWOT and Competition Analysis Exercise*	To identify the key strengths, weaknesses, opportunities, and threats, and ensure that the team understands the competition	Step 5
64	*Creating a One-page Business Plan and Then Some Exercise*	To create a business case and plan	Step 5
65	*Personal Branding Mad Libs® Exercise*	To self-reflect on our individual attributes, goals, and aspirations and learn how to create a personal branding statement and to effectively communicate your brand to connect with clients, pitch ideas, and influence stakeholders generally but also at ConPosium	KickOff Step 5 ConPosium

#	EXERCISE OR RESOURCE	PURPOSE	TIMING
66	*Powerful Presencing Tips Resource*	To provide tips for how to best present and own the stage without upstaging your teammates	Step 5 ConPosium
67	*Pre-Mortem Exercise*	To prevent groupthink so that the more likely threats/weaknesses of a project are identified early on	Step 5
68	*Rehearsals Dos and Don'ts and Q&A Tips Resource*	To provide tips on how to run rehearsals so that they are effective and help the teams move forward, and to provide tips on how to answer questions and respond to judges' feedback	Step 5 ConPosium
69	*Sample Business Plans Resource*	To provide examples of business plans	Step 5
70	*Show Don't Tell, 5 Parts of Effective Storytelling Exercise*[16]	To help teams create beautiful decks and present their Projects of Worth	Step 5 ConPosium
71	*Storytelling and Scripting "Challenger Sale" Exercise*[17]	To help teams create moving stories, and a succinct, compelling script	Step 5 ConPosium
72	*Storytelling, Scripting, and Deck Development Tips Resource*	To provide tips to teams for how to create beautiful decks, moving stories, and a succinct compelling script	Step 5 ConPosium
73	*Superhero Presentation Power Tricks Exercise*	To share what each team member individually does immediately before a presentation to get revved up and ready so teammates can exapt other teammates' tips to source the energy they need to rock the final presentation	Step 5 ConPosium

© Michele DeStefano

[16] This exercise was developed by Anita Ritchie, the Director of LawWithoutWalls.

[17] Phyllis Dealy and I adapted this exercise from *The Challenger Sale*, https://repeatablesuccess.com/2013/01/19/challenger-sale-reframe-exercise/.

Acknowledgments

I owe a great deal of thanks to many, many people for helping me with this book. I thank all of my readers who read this handbook and *Leader Upheaval* (at the same time) and provided suggested edits along with their endorsements! You can find the names of the readers in the *Praise for the Leader Upheaval Handbook* section at the beginning of this handbook. I also thank Anita Ritchie and Tiffany Perez for their helpful comments and suggested revisions to the various versions that they read and re-read. I thank the students that helped me with my citations (Annemarie Machado, Caitlin McNulty, Allie Simon, and Josh Schulster). I thank everyone on the LawWithoutWalls MiamiLaw team for their patience while I wrote and edited this book including Claire Amador, Elizabeth Castano, Katherine Miranda, Priscilla Ruiz, and Jaclyn Marie Sanchez. I thank the LawWithoutWalls community and all the teams that I have led and learned from during their 3-4-5 Journey to a Project of Worth. And, of course, I thank my editors and publisher without whom this book would not be published. Thank you to Stuart Horwitz, my tireless partner in helping me rewrite and restructure this handbook and *Leader Upheaval* over and over again. Thank you to Joanne Creary, Lynn Gohn, and Lorraine Murray for their patience and detail-oriented edits. Lastly, I thank my family and especially my significant other, Ian Norris, for putting up with my long nights and busy weekends as I wrote this handbook and *Leader Upheaval* over the past year!

About the Author

Michele DeStefano is a highly innovative and accomplished legal professional with a passion for creative problem-solving, collaboration, culture change, and innovation in law. As a Professor at the University of Miami who teaches at the Law School and School of Engineering, a visiting faculty member at Harvard Law School, and a Faculty Chair in Harvard Law School's Executive Education Program, Michele is an internationally recognized thought leader who has been named a Legal Rebel by the ABA and one of the top 20 most innovative lawyers in North America by the Financial Times Innovative Lawyers.

Michele is the founder of LawWithoutWalls, a community of over 2,000 lawyers, business professionals, entrepreneurs, and students who collaborate to create innovations in the business of law and develop new mindsets and skillsets. She is also the co-creator of the *Compliance-Elliance Journal*, and the Digital Legal Exchange, a nonprofit that aims to inspire general counsel and their teams to become digital leaders in their businesses to drive commercial value.

With her extensive research and writing on topics such as client-centricity, collaboration, and innovation in law, Michele has authored multiple books, including *Legal Upheaval: A Guide to Creativity, Collaboration, and Innovation in Law*; *New Suits: Appetite for Disruption*; and upcoming books, *Leader Upheaval: A Guide to Client-Centricity, Culture Creation, and Collaboration*; and *The Leader Upheaval Handbook: Lead Teams with The 3-4-5 Method™ of Innovation*. Michele has also written numerous articles, some of which include: *Chicken or Egg: Diversity and Innovation in the Corporate Legal Marketplace* (published in the *Fordham Law Review*) and *Don't Let the Digital Tail Wag the Transformation Dog: A Digital Transformation Roadmap for Corporate Counsel* (published in the *Journal of Business and Technology Law*).

Michele earned her Bachelor of Arts degree magna cum laude from Dartmouth College and her Juris Doctorate degree magna cum laude from Harvard Law School. Michele is a true visionary who is dedicated to leading the way in transforming the professional services industry. She frequently speaks and runs workshops on creative problem solving, collaboration, client-centricity, communication, personal branding, and innovation. For more information visit movelaw.com or micheledestefano.com.

Index

Note: Page numbers followed by an "f" refer to figures.